Cryptocurrency - 2021

A Complete Introduction to Blockchain & Cryptocurrencies

(Bitcoin, Litecoin, Ethereum, Cardano, Polkadot, Bitcoin Cash, Stellar, Tether, Monero, Dogecoin and More...)

CW01024012

Introduction

2021 edition.

Blockchain is the technology that enables the existence of cryptocurrencies. Bitcoin is the name of the best-known cryptocurrency; the one for which blockchain technology was invented.

A cryptocurrency is a medium of exchange, such as the US dollar, British Pound, or Euro, but is digital and uses encryption techniques to control the creation of monetary units and to verify the transfer of funds.

This is the descriptive introduction to Cryptocurrencies and Blockchain technology. The 160 pages in this book explain the technology and various cryptocurrencies, including Bitcoin, Ethereum, Ripple, Tether, Polkadot, Cardano, Stellar, Litecoin, Bitcoin Cash, and Dogecoin.

Table of Contents

Enjoy all our books for free...

  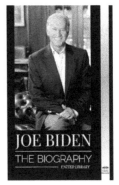

Interesting biographies, engaging introductions, and more.

Join the exclusive United Library reviewers club!

You will get a new book delivered in your inbox every Friday.

Join us today, go to: https://campsite.bio/unitedlibrary

Cryptomonnaie

A **cryptomoney,** also known as a **crypto-currency, cryptodevice, cryptographic currency** or **cybermoney** is a currency issued peer-to-peer, without the need for a central bank, usable by means of a decentralized computer network. It uses the principles of cryptography and involves the user in the process of issuing and settling transactions.

Principles of operation

Proof of work

Cryptomoney companies use a validation system such as proof of work to protect them from electronic forgeries. Several varieties of cryptosystems have been developed since the first one was introduced in 2009: the bitcoin,,,,,,,.

With few exceptions, the majority of cryptomoney systems are designed to create new units of money gradually, while setting, for most of them, a ceiling on the money supply that will eventually be in circulation. Compared to currencies with legal tender issued by financial institutions or held in cash, cryptomoney systems are managed by a register that can be consulted by anyone and which lists all transactions from the outset. Transactions are in principle supposed to be forgery-proof and tamper-proof, thanks to the intensive use of cryptography. Note that there are exceptions to the rule of anonymity, such as Monero, Dash, Zerocoin,,,,, Bytecoin and Black Coin.

Block generation and crypto-monetary creation by mining

When a transaction is issued, it is transmitted and validated by the computers that make up the network. This validation results from a calculation in which any person can participate. As soon as a transaction is validated, each computer that has participated in its validation is allocated an amount of cryptography in proportion to its participation in the calculation. Participating in the calculation of cryptography transactions requires a significant investment, since it is essential to invest in specialized systems such as FPGA or ASIC. Other cryptomoney systems based on different algorithms allow less powerful systems to participate in the calculation. Indeed GPUs, or CPUs for some cryptosystems, are powerful enough to perform calculations quickly. The participation in the creation of money, called "mining", follows a logarithmic scheme that aims to reproduce the discovery of gold :

- In the beginning, few people look for gold, so finding it is relatively simple.
- Then as information spreads and more and more people search, gold becomes more and more difficult to find and increasingly rare.
- As a result, the investment of actors is increasingly important, pushing the limits and forcing small researchers to give up.
- Because the resource is exhaustible and increasingly expensive to obtain, its value increases while its chance of discovery decreases.

Mature cryptosystems reach phases where complexity requires a sustained investment in hardware. New cryptosystems, or those that have not yet reached a sufficient volume, are still in their launch phase. Block generation raises the question of the energy spent to create cryptography. Depending on hardware configurations, power consumption can be high. Joining a group of block generators remains the most adequate method to pool resources and to obtain revenues from the mining activity. Cryptonics have variable efficiency ratios . Indeed, secondary cryptomoney systems, such as Monero or

Ethereum, being less widespread, block generation is more accessible and less competitive. Other cryptocurrencies, such as Gridcoin, donate part of the computation to scientific projects.

History of Cryptonry

Origin of the term cryptomony

The term "cryptomoney" is based on the encryption mechanism associated with this currency of a particular nature: "hidden").

1998-2009: the origins, a confidential diffusion

The concept of cryptography is a concept that existed long before the creation of Bitcoin. The company, DigiCash Inc., founded in 1989 by David Chaum, was founded with the goal of creating the first virtual currency to be used worldwide. DigiCash was a virtual currency company. It created an anonymous payment protocol based on cryptography. Nevertheless Digicash failed in its project of massive adoption of its cryptomony. The company was forced to declare bankruptcy in 1998.

In 1998, Wei Dai published a description of "b-money", an anonymous electronic cash system. Shortly thereafter, Nick Szabo created "Bit Gold," which required users to complete a proof-of-work function whose solutions were encrypted, bundled and published. Bitcoin, created in 2009 by a developer using the pseudonym of Satoshi Nakamoto uses the SHA-256 algorithm as a proof of work system. Other cryptomoney systems include Litecoin, Peercoin and Namecoin. Several other cryptomoney systems have been created: not all have been successful, especially those that are not very innovative.

2011-2017: the adoption of three generations of cryptosystems by a wide audience

During the first years of their existence, cryptomoney gradually gained the attention of the media and the public. Since 2011, interest has increased rapidly, especially during the rapid rise in the price of Bitcoin in April 2013. From 2014, a second generation of cryptosystems has emerged, such as Monero, Ethereum and Nxt with new features such as stealth addresses, smart contracts, the use of side block chains or backed by physical assets such as gold. Representatives of several central banks have stated that the use of cryptosystems poses significant challenges to economic equilibrium. In particular, from the point of view of the price of credit. They also felt that the growing popularity of commercial cryptomoney may lead to a loss of consumer confidence in fiat currencies. Gareth Murphy, a U.S. central bank representative, said that "widespread use would make it more difficult for statistical agencies to collect data on economic activity, which are themselves used by governments to guide the economy. He warned that cryptomoney poses a new challenge to the control of the important monetary and exchange rate policy functions of central banks.

The 1st, 2nd and 3rd generation cryptomoney :

1. The first generation is represented by Bitcoin . Solidly implanted, initiator of the media and public craze for cryptomoney, it suffers from regularly pointed shortcomings, such as its slowness, its relatively small block size, in particular.
2. A second generation presents either minor improvements or technological innovations allowing new functions. The archetype of this second generation is the Ethereum, which makes use of intelligent contracts.
3. The third generation: in response to new limitations, particularly in terms of capacity, security and governance, new cryptosystems have emerged, including the most well-known, such as EOS.IO,

Cardano , AION, ICON and Raiden Network . EOS.IO is itself derived from Ethereum. They bring innovations, but as of August 2018, none of them has taken the lead over the others.

The first stablecoin, bitUSD, is introduced in 2014. The launch of cryptoskills with a fixed price is based on the advantages claimed by this type of currency .

An entrepreneur, founder of Robocoin, launched the first bitcoin vending machine in the United States on February 20, 2014. The kiosk, located in Austin, Texas, is similar to a bank machine, but has scanners to read ID cards to confirm the identity of users.

In 2018, the market is down compared to its end of year 2017. However, the number of job offers in the sector continues to grow.

On August 21, 2019, employees of the South Ukrainian nuclear power plant who connected it to the internet to undermine cryptography were arrested by the secret service.

Types of Cryptosystems

By the end of 2019 there will be nearly 2,400 cryptomoney stores on the coinmarketcap site. Among these cryptomoney systems, certain types can be distinguished.

The Stablecoins

Stablecoins are intended to replicate the value of an asset, the dollar, gold or the euro. The objective is to avoid being subject to market volatility.

Notable stable corners include :

- Tether
- Dai
- Paxos

Stable corners are considered by central banks as potentially affecting financial stability, but also undermining monetary sovereignty. The Financial Stability Forum proposes to frame and regulate the stable corners, at least those which, by their global and universal nature, pose a problem in terms of financial risks. This recommendation follows the G7 position in 2019.

Applicable tax regime

Cryptonics experienced a period of relative legal uncertainty before the legislator intervened in the vote on the 2019 finance law.

The first regime comes into force with the tax instruction of July 11, 2014: cryptomoney is then qualified as "*virtual units of account stored on an electronic medium*", taxable under the progressive scale of income tax, in the category of non-commercial profits.

The second regime comes into force with the ruling handed down by the Conseil d'Etat on April 26, 2018: cryptomoney is qualified as "intangible movable property" within the meaning of civil property law, taxable in the category of capital gains on movable property under article 150 UA of the CGI, or failing that, non-commercial profits or industrial and commercial profits . In addition to the social security contributions, a flat rate of 12.9% was applied to the capital gain, which also benefited from a tax exemption for any transfer of less than €5,000.

The current regime, voted with the Finance Act of December 28, 2018, defines cryptomoney as digital assets in Article L54-10-1 of the French Monetary and Financial Code: digital assets are civilly intangible personal property, taxable for income tax purposes, on the basis of Article 150 VH bis of the General Tax Code. Capital gains from the sale of digital assets are subject to the same single flat-rate tax as income from movable assets: a flat rate of 12.8% to which must be added 17.2% social security contributions. A tax exemption applies when the gross annual amount of the disposals is less than €305.

Declaration of any account held on a platform

Since January 1, 2020, any account opened, held or closed on a digital asset exchange platform or intermediary must be declared at the same time as the taxpayer completes his tax return: form 3916 bis, a different form from form 3916, provided for traditional foreign bank accounts, must be completed.

Legal framework for fundraising: ICO

Initial coin offering, in reference to proposals for equity securities by stock exchanges, is a form of financing, halfway between fundraising and equity financing, through the pre-sale of a new cryptomony. The first notable Initial coin offering is that of Ethereum in 2014.

In 2017, this market is still poorly regulated, so in September China bans ICOs on its territory. In Russia, Vladimir Putin approves the use of ICOs by demanding the implementation of appropriate regulations to control the cryptomoney market.

A *Security Token Offering* or STO is an *Initial Coin Offering* framed by legal standards.

Some cryptomonnages

Cryptomoney of sovereign states

- In January 2018, the Bank of England announced that it wanted to create a cryptomony system indexed to the British currency·
- In Canada and Singapore, institutions are also planning to develop official payment systems in cryptography.
- In 2018, the Marshall Islands becomes the first country in the world to launch a legal cryptography system.
- In 2018, Venezuelan President Nicolas Maduro created a cryptomony, the petro, pegged to the price of a barrel of oil, in order to circumvent U.S. sanctions.
- In 2018, Turkey is also considering its currency, Turkcoin, to boost the economy.

- In 2018, Iran plans to create a national cryptomony, based on bitcoin, to counter the fall of the national currency due to the return of American sanctions.
- In 2019, the People's Republic of China considers that it is about to launch its cryptonics to suppress cash, after having initiated the movement in 2014 and filed 80 patents. It is called DCEP or Digital Currency Electronic Payment.

Main exchange platforms

Active

- Bittrex
- Binance
- Bitstamp
- BTER
- Coinbase
- Gatecoin
- Kraken
- Poloniex

Inactive

- Mt. Gox
- Cryptsy
- Vault of Satoshi

Features, advantages and disadvantages

Benefits

- Designed for the Internet, they offer alternatives to payment systems based on legal tender currencies.

They increase the accessibility of e-commerce in developing countries.

- Transparency: all transactions are public, with the owners and recipients of these transactions identified by addresses.
- Cryptomoney cannot be counterfeited or usurped. The encryption protocol is also designed to be highly resistant against most known computer threats, including distributed denial of service attacks.
- Transfer fees are sometimes zero and lower than those of payment institutions or money transfer companies .
- Fast transfers from a few seconds to a few minutes compared to bank transfers .
- Transfers are possible worldwide regardless of country.
- No intermediary: the amount credited is charged directly to the receiving address.
- Any individual or company can transfer cryptography.
- Remote storage of the cryptomonnaie on a server or downloading on a support .
- For some cryptomoney, the total quantity that can be created is capped, making this type of currency essentially deflationary.

Disadvantages

- Low impact of cryptomoney on the general public .
- Poorly developed payment network although growing.
- Different cryptomoney, incompatible with each other, with the development of several types of cryptomoney in parallel.
- High volatility.
- Risk of deflation/hyperinflation due to insufficient or too much money creation.
- Security required: password, double authentication.

- Illegality in some countries.
- Lost cryptomony is definitely lost.
- Increasing energy consumption due to mining activities.

Other features :

- Currencies not dependent on central banks.
- Irreversibility of transactions: the receiver of the currency cannot be cancelled. Conversely, the originator cannot retract his payment.
- Banking lobby opposing the use of this type of currency and defending payment systems using legal tender currencies.
- Lack of ceiling and minimum in transfers.

Blockchain

A **blockchain,** or **chain of blocks** is a technology for the storage and transmission of information without a control device. Technically, it is a distributed database whose information sent by users and internal links within the database are checked and grouped at regular time intervals into blocks, thus forming a chain. The whole is secured by cryptography. By extension, a chain of blocks is a distributed database that manages a list of records protected against tampering or modification by storage nodes; it is therefore a secure, distributed record of all transactions carried out since the start of the distributed system.

There is an analogy with the Internet, because in both cases the technologies use computer protocols linked to a decentralized infrastructure. The Internet allows packets of data to be transferred from a "secure" server to remote clients, while a *blockchain* allows "trust" to be established between separate agents in the system. With *blockchain* technology, the "trusted third party" becomes the system itself: each distributed element of the *blockchain* contains the elements necessary to guarantee the integrity of the data exchanged.

Aspects

Previous work

The first study on cryptographically secure block strings was described in 1991 by Stuart Haber and W. Scott Stornetta. They wanted to implement a system where time-stamped documents could not be falsified or backdated. In 1992, Bayer, Haber and Stornetta incorporated the Merkle Tree concept into the system, which improved its efficiency by allowing multiple documents to be assembled into a single block.

According to researcher Ittai Abraham, the first decentralized certification system is that of the Surety company, which has published a cryptographic certificate from its database every week since 1995 in the "Ads and Lost & Found" section of the *New York Times*.

The first chain of blocks was conceptualized by a person known as Satoshi Nakamoto in 2008. It was implemented the following year by Nakamoto as the main component of Bitcoin, where it serves as the public registry for all transactions on the network.

Historical and societal aspects

Many virtual currencies and crypto-currencies use block strings for their security. Satoshi Nakamoto, the inventor of Bitcoin, was the first to apply a decentralized block chain. Transactions on a block chain are very difficult to reverse because block chains are resistant to change.

Energy and environmental aspects

The consumption of electricity and IT resources are among the hidden transaction costs of the blockchain.

A study conducted in 2014 by two Irish researchers shows that systems based on the proof-of-work *blockchain* concept can be described as energy chasms. The use of proof of work induces an exponentially increasing consumption of electricity and computing time worldwide; this is why the Bank for International Settlements has criticized the system of proof of work validations necessary for the blockchain; a system qualified as an environmental disaster by Hyun Song Shin in June 2018....

Nicholas Weaver , after examining the online safety of the blockchain and the energy efficiency of the "proof of work" system used by the blockchains, concludes in both cases that these solutions are "totally inadequate".

The Ethereum protocol plans to reduce the energy and ecological cost of the blockchain by replacing the proof-of-work mining process with a proof-of-stake mining process. The date for this change has not yet been set.

Legal aspects

The chain of blocks raises legal issues. These questions relate to various issues: competition law, privacy law, intellectual property law, contract law and the governance of the chain.

In particular, blockchains with public governance operate without a trusted third party, corresponding to a form of community idealism. They differ from consortium blockchains where the nodes participating in the consensus are defined in advance, as in the R3 project.

A private blockchain works with an established framework whose rules, possibly extrinsic to the code, govern its operation, whereas the public blockchain does not define any other rule than that of the code constituted by the protocol and software technology that composes it.

With regard to the right to privacy, the CNIL produces a report in 2018 indicating that blockchains are not a priori problematic, except with regard to the exercise of the right to erase personal data, which is part of the principles of the RGPD, for example.

How it works

The proof of work, the historical method of consensus

The chain of blocks is a form of implementation of the solution of the "Byzantine Generals Problem". This mathematical problem consists in ensuring that a set of computer components working together can handle failures and produce a consensus. The system must be able to maintain its reliability in the event that a minority of the components send erroneous or malicious information, as in the case of cryptography, in order to bypass the verification of double spending by the network miners.

The historical method for reaching this type of consensus is "proof of work". This method uses a mathematical problem whose solution makes it possible to verify that the "miner" has actually done a job. The protocol uses a cryptographic system based on a decentralized system of proofs: the resolution of the proof requires a high level of computing power provided by the miners. Minors are entities whose role is to supply the network with computing power, to enable the decentralized database to be updated. For this update, the miners must confirm the new blocks by validating the data. In the case of bitcoin and in the case of adding blocks to the string, a brute force cryptography problem must be solved in order to add a new block. Depending on the "difficulty" of the chain at the time of resolution, the chain may need to be repeated several hundred billion times. In the case of Bitcoin, a miner is only paid for his work if he was the first to solve the cryptographic problem.

There is competition among miners for the addition of new blocks, but also a certain solidarity. Anyone can lend their computing power to mine, but the more miners there are, the greater the "difficulty" and the more difficult it is to solve the cryptographic problem. Conversely, if miners stop mining, the difficulty decreases. The protocol can become almost inviolable as soon as no group of miners becomes the majority.

Among the pitfalls associated with this method are: the latency time required to validate a transaction and the decreasing profit of the miners. The significant energy consumption associated with this method is also pointed out. Faced with these observations, the "blockchain" community is debating the use of consensus methods that would no longer be proof of work but, for example, proof of participation.

Other methods of consensus

Several entities use other methods of consensus. For example, Peercoin's crypto-currency uses a mixture of "proof of work" and "proof of participation", i.e. it adapts the difficulty of the work according to the "share" of each of the nodes. Participation" is defined as the product of the number of peercoins held and the age of each of these nodes. The higher the participation, the more the difficulty of the hash function is reduced; this mechanically reduces the energy consumption of the mining algorithms required to create money.

Ethereum, which uses the "proof of work" method, announced in 2015 its decision to gradually migrate to proof of participation in 2018 or 2019.

The Burstcoin uses a proof of storage, where hard disks store "traces", whose presence is proven by accessing them. This protocol is distinguished by its low power consumption.

Governance

It is important to note that the notion of *Law* in blockchains should not be understood in the sense of legislative laws, but of a law *internal to the* process of the blockchain, managed by the governance of the blockchain. The usual phrase "*Code is Law*" regularly used as a rule of governance of blockchains therefore does not refer to national or international laws, but only to the "rules of governance" enacted and applicable to the Blockchain. In this case, these laws are often only computer codes and algorithms, so that the rules enacted can be verified by minors during transaction verification sessions. Any transaction that respects the codes is accepted in the Blockchain, otherwise the modification is rejected, without human intervention of the governance .

Several modes of governance are possible:

- An 'open' mode. In this case, as a general rule, the law applicable to the chain is the law designated by the parties.
- A 'semi-closed' mode. This can be used for functions assigned to states or institutions managing secure data. In this case, the rules are

freer, as the central body has control over the technical aspects of validating the Blockchain.

- a closed mode . In this case, the interest lies in the theoretical robustness and traceability of the process, which does not need to be public, but which needs this security. Note that in this case, it remains vulnerable to a 51% attack, due to the non-decentralization and non-publication.

Open governance does not mean no governance. In the case of Bitcoin, which accounts for 50% of the total value of the cryptoskills in circulation as of August 18, 2018, governance is provided by the community in a decentralized manner. Decentralization is a major contribution of the blockchain and, by ricochet, of the cryptocurrencies. There is a wiki, IRC discussion forums dedicated to governance, technology, etc., and even an emergency protocol in case of hacking or a proven bug. Of course, what is available for Bitcoin is not necessarily available or applicable for other cryptosystems, especially the newer and/or more confidential ones.

Organization

Management science researchers are studying the role of block chains in supporting different forms of collaboration. Block chains can foster both cooperation and coordination. Through the reliability, transparency, traceability of records, and immutability of information, block chains facilitate collaboration in a way that differs from both the traditional use of contracts and relational standards. Unlike contracts, block chains do not rely directly on the legal system to enforce agreements. In addition, unlike the use of relational norms, block chains do not require trust or direct relationships between collaborators.

Transactions

Transactions represent exchanges between users, which are stored within the blocks of the block chain.

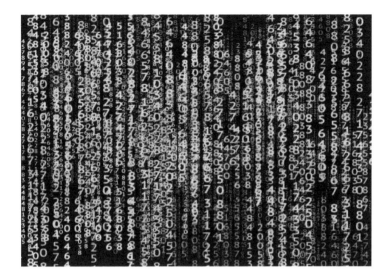

Blocks

The various transactions recorded are grouped in blocks. After recording recent transactions, a new block is generated and all transactions will be validated by the miners, who will analyze the complete history of the block chain. If the block is valid, it is time-stamped and added to the block chain. The transactions it contains are then visible in the whole network. Once added to the chain, a block cannot be modified or deleted, which guarantees the authenticity and security of the network.

Each block of the chain consists of the following elements :

- several transactions ;
- a checksum, used as an identifier;
- the checksum of the previous block ;

- a measure of the amount of work that was required to produce the block. This is defined by the consensus method used in the chain, such as "proof of work" or "proof of participation".

Applications

The flagship application of this technology is that of crypto-currencies such as Bitcoin, for example, which is however far from being the only virtual currency: there are many others such as Ether, Monero, and dozens of others more or less confidential.

Beyond its monetary aspect, this technology of decentralized information storage could have multiple applications requiring secure exchanges without going through a centralizing body, or traceability that cannot be falsified, such as :

- applications based on intelligent contracts, allowing the exchange of all kinds of goods or services ;
- ways to reduce payment and transaction costs. International banks made announcements in 2015 on these subjects. Twenty-five of them have, for example, signed a partnership with an American company R3 for the use of *blockchains in the* financial markets. Citibank has also announced its wish to issue its own cryptomonnaise, the Citicoin. Similarly, in April 2015, the UBS bank opened its own research laboratory in London dedicated to the study of *blockchain* technology and its applications in the financial field. Through this research and these consortiums, the banks hope to implement a *blockchain-based* technology that will become a reference in the banking field. Indeed, the consortium or bank that is the first to release a

proven technology will be able to charge its own service to other financial players;
- Means to improve their predictive systems called "oracles", especially for the insurance industry;
- the development of *peer-to-peer* insurance;
- the traceability of products in the food chain·.

In terms of participatory financing, the blockchain has enabled the implementation of ICO, which allows for extremely rapid fundraising.

The technology is being developed in Ghana by the NGO Bitland to create a virtual cadastre. A similar project had been envisaged for a while in Honduras but was not finally successful. Georgia has also announced a cadastre experiment on the block in partnership with the Bitcoin start-up BitFury, as well as Sweden with the start-up ChromaWay.

The industrial group General Electric has chosen to invest in a start-up called Xage, which uses the blockchain to create digital footprints of industrial machines and thus identify and secure each machine in an electrical network.

From the very first years, experts warned against the possible overuse of block chains. For example, in 2018, the National Institute of Standards and Technology presents a report indicating that many problems are best solved with databases or simple emails.

The blockchain system is also used to provide an information storage system that preserves privacy and places it in "user hands" rather than in the hands of a third party· and to circumvent the censorship of centralized systems such as Google / Youtube. For example, the brave browsers co-founded by Brendan Eich or dissenter, or the video platform Verasity.

Initiatives around the world

In Europe

In May 2016, the European Parliament validated the creation of a working group to monitor the *blockchain* and crypto-currencies. This group will be steered by the European Commission and its objective is to monitor these technologies and recommend legislative measures. On February [1,] 2018 the European Commission launches, with the support of the European Parliament, the EU Blockchain Observatory Forum. Its missions are to highlight major developments in block chain technology, to encourage European actors in this sector and to help strengthen European engagement with several stakeholders active in this field.

In Germany

On June 28, 2017, Landesbank Baden-Württemberg and the automotive manufacturer Daimler AG announced that they have used blockchain technology for the first time to execute a financial transaction. Daimler launched a 100 million euro Schuldschein over the course of one year in which four savings banks acted as lenders. The entire transaction was carried out using *blockchain* technology in cooperation with the respective IT subsidiaries of the two protagonists.

In Spain

The BBVA bank is studying the use of the *blockchain in the* case of imports/exports between America and Europe.

In Switzerland

The Canton of Geneva is conducting a pilot project for the issuance of electronic extracts from the Commercial Register with Ethereum and in the commodities trade in a public-private partnership. The city of Zug is also conducting a pilot project to develop a digital identity for its population.

In the Netherlands

Development of regional collaborative projects .

In Estonia

The state has created an e-resident system using blockchain technology.

In Canada

In the Canadian province of Quebec, the accounting firm Raymond Chabot Grant Thornton announced in July 2017 the launch of catallaxy , a center of expertise on blockchain technology with experts in the field, Jonathan Hamel, Francis Pouliot and Vincent Gauthier. The name Catallaxy is a reference to the importance of spontaneous order and other concepts of the Austrian School of Economics in Bitcoin.

In Asia

In Asia, a consortium comprising the Monetary Authority of Singapore and eight other banks was formed in November 2016 for a pilot project to implement a platform based on this type of decentralized digital transaction registry. As a first step, banks will be able to purchase virtual currency under the control of the MAS. This currency can then be used either for interbank payments or exchanged for real rather than virtual currency. A second phase plans to include transactions in foreign currencies.

In Israel

In 2017, the Israeli company Zim conducted an experiment of digital bill of lading using the blockchain.

Bitcoin

Bitcoin is a cryptomoney otherwise known as cryptographic currency. In the case of the unit denomination, it is written "Bitcoin" and in the case of the peer-to-peer payment system it is written "Bitcoin". The idea was first presented in November 2008 by a person, or a group of persons, under the pseudonym Satoshi Nakamoto. The source code for the reference implementation was released in 2009.

The G20 considers Bitcoin to be "crypto-active". The term "crypto-active" then refers to "virtual assets stored on an electronic medium allowing a community of users accepting them as payment to carry out transactions without having to resort to legal tender".

Presentation

How it works

To create and manage Bitcoins, Bitcoin relies on software. In this software, Bitcoins are created according to a protocol that pays the agents who have processed transactions.

These agents use their computing power to verify, secure and record the transactions in a virtual registry, called the blockchain, a name that comes from the fact that the basic entity of Bitcoin is called a block, and that the blocks are then linked together in a chain, the block chain.

For each new block accepted, the *verification-security-recording* activity, called *mining,* is paid for by newly created bitcoins and by the fees of the transactions processed. As a currency or commodity, Bitcoins can be exchanged for other currencies or commodities, goods or services. The exchange rate for cryptomoney is set in specialized marketplaces and fluctuates according to the law of supply and demand.

It is possible to buy Bitcoins online on specialized platforms, physical terminals or in exchange for any good or service with a person who already owns one. The platforms also allow to follow in real time the evolution of the price of Bitcoin compared to other currencies or cryptomoney.

Unit of account

The unit of account of Bitcoin is *Bitcoin*. Its issuance is limited to 20,999,999.977 units, each divisible to eight decimal places . The official currency symbol has been deposited and accepted in 2015 with Unicode . The corresponding acronyms, used by the exchange platforms, are BTC and XBT. Among the unofficial symbols used are ฿ and Ƀ.

Decentralization

The system operates without a central authority or a single administrator. It is managed in a decentralized way thanks to the consensus of all the nodes of the network. Bitcoin is the largest decentralized cryptographic currency, with a capitalization of $545 billion as of January [1,] 2021 .

Means of payment

As a means of payment, Bitcoin is being accepted by a growing number of merchants, encouraged by transaction fees that are generally lower than the 2-3% charged by credit card organizations and independent of the amount of the financial transaction. However, in 2017, the fees increased significantly in a few months, from $0.2 in 2016 to $20 on certain days in December 2017, so that the Steam platform or Microsoft withdrew Bitcoin as a means of payment, precisely because of excessively high transaction fees . In order to solve the problem of too high transaction fees, the progressive deployment of various technological improvements throughout 2018 and 2019 allowed fees to drop to around $0.05 for non-urgent transactions, and even to amounts below $0.0001 for Lightning type transactions. Unlike credit cards, any fees are not charged to the seller but to the buyer, who chooses to pay them voluntarily. A Bitcoin transaction is irrevocable and cannot be cancelled. Despite a 500% growth in the number of merchants accepting Bitcoin in 2014, cryptography is not well established in the retail sector, but continues to gain a foothold in trade.

Usage

Between January 2009 and March 2010, the use of Bitcoin was a hobby among crypto enthusiasts, and Bitcoin had no real value. However, in April 2010, Bitcoin started trading in an exchange for 0.003 USD, and shortly afterwards, in May 2010, it already had a value of 0.01 USD, and a few months later, July 2010 added 0.08 USD again. These, although they were very low prices and their actual use as a means of payment was very low, reflect the rapid rise in prices that this zero value 10-cent crypto-currency has experienced.

From its creation in 2009 until the closure of Silk Road by the US authorities in 2013, Bitcoin was used mainly as a medium of exchange by criminal networks for gambling, the purchase of illegal substances, or for pirated databases. Cryptography has attracted the attention of financial authorities, legislative bodies in various countries, particularly in the United States, and the media.

Nevertheless, in recent years, cryptomoney has matured and a growing number of studies conclude that these illegal activities, although they still exist as in any payment system, now represent only a minority share of the exchanges of cryptomoney. The U.S. Senate also recognizes that Bitcoin can be used to provide perfectly legitimate financial services.

Safe haven value

According to some experts, Bitcoin is more of a safe haven than a means of payment, although unlike gold, Bitcoin can indeed be used for both purposes. Conversely, other financial experts consider Bitcoin to be far too volatile to be a safe haven, but it has only been around since 2009 and its possible safe haven status will only be possible after an initial period of intense volatility. Whether Bitcoin can reach the market value of gold is still much debated, hence the volatility of Bitcoin.

Since March 2020, the value of Bitcoin has only been rising, it is tending towards its highest historical quotation. On January 7, 2021, its value exceeded $40,000 for the first time.

History

Creation

Bitcoin is an improvement of the concept of *b-money,* imagined by Wei Dai in 1999, and *bitgold*, described in 2005 by Nick Szabo. In particular, Bitcoin solves the crucial problem of the trust model: servers considered serious vote with their computing power to determine the legitimate transaction chain. In b-money, servers were supposed to pay a security deposit according to a mechanism that is not very explicit. The idea of using a chain of computational proofs was put forward in the bitgold project, although Nick Szabo proposed to use only a majority of addresses to establish the legitimacy of a transaction chain, leaving the problem of controlling the number of addresses intact.

Satoshi Nakamoto said he worked on Bitcoin from 2007 to 2009. As early as 2008, he published a paper on a mailing list describing Bitcoin digital currency. In February 2009, he posted an announcement about his work on the P2P Foundation website. On January 3, 2009, the first block or *genesis* block is created. In February 2009, he releases the first version of the Bitcoin software on the P2P Foundation website and to make the network work, he uses his computer to generate the first Bitcoins. With other developers, Nakamoto continues the implementation of the software and its *Bitcoin-Qt* version until 2010.

Developers and the Bitcoin community are gradually losing contact with him in mid-2010. On December 12, 2010, a last message is posted by Nakamoto on the main forum. Shortly before passing away, Nakamoto appointed Gavin Andresen as his successor, giving him access to the Bitcoin SourceForge project and a copy of the alert key. The latter is a unique private cryptographic key that can be used to mitigate the effects of a potential attack on the Bitcoin system, such as the discovery of a cryptographic flaw allowing transactions to be modified a *posteriori,* or the takeover of more than 51% of the nodes on the network.

The operators of the network nodes can either warn their users or stop all transaction recording during an alert.

On September 27, 2012, the Bitcoin Foundation is created. Important figures from the world of new technologies very quickly supported the project, such as Wences Casares.

Satoshi Nakamoto's identity

Several people claimed to be *Satoshi Nakamoto,* but none of them could prove it. There is no record of his identity prior to the creation of Bitcoin. On his profile, Satoshi claimed to be a 40-year-old Japanese man.

In March 2014, journalist Leah McGrath Goodman of *Newsweek* magazine announced that she has tracked down the inventor of Bitcoin, who she believes is a 64-year-old Japanese American whose birth name is "Satoshi Nakamoto", although he changed his name to "Dorian Prentice Satoshi Nakamoto" at the age of 23, and is a retired physicist living in California. This thesis was methodically disassembled a month later by linguists at Aston University in England, who conducted an in-depth study of the linguistic correspondences between the written productions of the author of the Bitcoin white paper and several suspected personalities, including Dorian Nakamoto.

Satoshi's way of writing on the forums and in the whitepaper suggests that he would be British.

In 2016, Craig Steven Wright, an Australian entrepreneur, claims to be Satoshi Nakamoto. However, strong doubts remain, as he himself declared on May 5, 2016, in an enigmatic post on his personal blog, to renounce to disseminate the evidence confirming that he is indeed the creator of Bitcoin.

Acceptance

On November 16, 2012, WordPress will accept Bitcoins for its paid services.

On November 28, 2012, miners' wages will decrease for the first time from 50 to 25 BTC. The Bitcoin source code provides for a halving of the remuneration, called halving, every two hundred and ten thousand mined blocks, approximately every four years.

On February 14, 2013, the Reddit community site will set up a system to buy "Reddit Gold" with bitcoins.

On February 16, 2013, the online storage site Mega, successor of Megaupload, accepts payments in bitcoin.

On October 14, 2013, the giant Baidu will accept bitcoin transactions for its Jiasule firewall service.

On November 21, 2013, the University of Nicosia announces that it will accept Bitcoin and open a Master's degree in Economics specializing in digital currencies.

On November 22, 2013, Richard Branson announced that Virgin Galactic will now accept Bitcoin as a means of payment for its space tourism flights.

On November 29, 2013, Jiangsu Telecom, a subsidiary of China Telecom, will now accept Bitcoin.

On March 25, 2014, the U.S. Internal Revenue Service will declare that Bitcoin is not to be considered as a currency, but as a commodity, the transactions of which are subject to capital gains tax. This means taking into account the exchange rate at which Bitcoin is acquired and the exchange rate at which it is used in order to calculate the realized capital gain, which makes the legal use of Bitcoin in the United States particularly difficult.

On May 9, 2014, the U.S. Election Commission agreed that election campaigns will be funded in Bitcoin up to a limit of $100 per election cycle.

On September 23, 2014, Paypal will allow selected digital merchants in North America selected by Bitcoin payment processor partners to accept Bitcoin payments, and is thus opening up very gradually to Bitcoin.

As of October 16, 2017, there were 1,686 distributors worldwide.

In November 2018, the Ohio government announced that it would accept tax payments in Bitcoins.

In January 2020, a study by investing.com reveals that 9% of financial advisors already invest part of their client's funds in Bitcoin to protect them from currency turbulence.

Notable Incidents

On August 15, 2010, a block is generated containing a transaction creating 184,467,440,737 bitcoins for three different addresses. This flaw is related to the fact that the code did not foresee the case of creating such large quantities of bitcoins. This problem was solved automatically by the bitcoin blockchain and these bitcoins no longer exist.

On March 12, 2013, an incident related to a non-retro compatibility of version 0.8.0 occurs: the chain splits into several versions and some remain blocked for a few hours.

On April 11, 2013, the value of bitcoin collapsed from $266 to $105 before stabilizing at $160 in less than six hours. On April 13, the price reaches €66. The price had increased eightfold in less than five weeks.

On October 2, 2013, Ross Ulbricht was arrested. He is the alleged founder of Silk Road, which is closed by the FBI and which used only Bitcoin for all its transactions.

On February 11, 2014, the Bitcoin network fell victim to a massive and concerted attack launched on numerous exchange platforms.

On February 24, 2014, the Mt. Gox trading platform suffered a record loss of 744,408 BTC, equivalent to more than 250 million euros. The website is temporarily closed. A crisis management document has been drafted and is publicly available. According to some specialized media, the future of bitcoin is threatened. The exchange rate remains stable on the other platforms. Bitcoin lost more than 38% of its value in the first quarter of 2014.

On September 11, 2015, Mark Karpelès, boss of the Mt. Gox platform, was indicted in Japan for embezzlement. He is suspected of having embezzled 2.3 million euros from bitcoin deposits. The suspect denies these accusations outright.

In May 2016, the Gatecoin exchange site is hacked and 250 bitcoins and 185,000 ether are stolen. The hacker managed to circumvent the online storage limits of the exchange platform's assets: while only 5% of the depots are not cold stored, the hacker managed to empty these depots while continuing to supply the address by transferring assets from the exchange platform's cold storage facilities.

On August 3, 2016, the Bitfinex exchange site reports a theft of 119,756 Bitcoins on its exchange platform, representing $65 million in crypto-money in July 2016.

On May 7, 2019, hackers stole more than 7,000 Bitcoins from the Binance Cryptocurrency Exchange, worth more than US$40 million. Binance CEO Zhao Changpeng said: "The hackers used a variety of techniques, including phishing, viruses and other attacks.... The hackers had the patience to wait and execute well-orchestrated actions through several seemingly independent accounts at the most opportune time." .

All incidents related to trading platforms only affect people who do not themselves hold the private keys to their Bitcoin portfolio. *Not your keys not your bitcoins*

Trojan Horse

The so-called Trojan Horse technique allows to change the address of the recipient of the crypto-money operation. CryptoShuffler is one of the softwares using this technique. This technique, which is rare, has little effect because it is enough for the sender of the payment to visually check the first/last characters of the destination address to make sure he is not being tricked.

Exchange rate trends against the dollar and the euro

When it was created in February 2009, cryptomoney was first exchanged only as an experiment by a few rare users and its value was nil. On October 12, 2009, the first known sale of Bitcoin took place, where two users exchanged 5,050 Bitcoins for 5.02 USD by Paypal transfer, which corresponds to a price of about 0.001 USD per Bitcoin.

In March 2010, *Bitcoinmarket.com* is the first Bitcoin trading platform to open, allowing a continuous quotation of the Bitcoin price.

On February 9, 2011, Bitcoin reaches parity with the dollar. On November 29, 2013, the value of one Bitcoin exceeds that of an ounce of gold, at nearly $1,250.

Bitcoin, which is mainly exchanged for yuans and dollars, can also be exchanged for euros on about ten platforms. Until November 2013, Mt. Gox was the most important of these platforms in terms of trading volume and it was customary to consider its price as representative of the market. Following the problems it encountered, users turned away from it, causing a sharp drop in the price of bitcoin on Mt. Gox, with prices on the other platforms being little affected.

2013

The share price increased by 400% between January and March 2013, before correcting severely on April 10, following the failure of the Mt. Gox exchange site and probable panic sales. The price then fell back to the previous month's level, to around USD 50. Between December 4 and 5, 2013, following a warning from the People's Bank of China and the Banque de France, the price lost nearly 35% in 24 hours.

2014

On February 19, 2014, the price collapses following the announcement of the disappearance of bitcoins on Mt. Gox. On this trading platform, Bitcoin fell from €185 on February 18 to €73 24 hours later, while it remained around €400 on the other platforms. Mt. Gox will declare bankruptcy on February 28, 2014. On May [1,] 2014, a group of investors called Sunlot Holdings proposed to buy the site for a symbolic bitcoin.

2016

In 2016, after the announcement of Brexit on June 24, the value of Bitcoin skyrocketed, gaining more than 9%, while all financial markets plunged for less than a week.

2017

On March 2, 2017, Bitcoin once again surpassed the value of an ounce of gold, reaching almost $1,300. The price fell in mid-March 2017, reaching less than $1,000 on March 18, 2017.

Bitcoin sees its value gradually rise during April 2017 and eventually exceeds USD 1,300 by the end of April. The value of Bitcoin rose sharply in May, surpassing $1,500 for the first time on May 4, 2017, reaching $2,000 on May 20, reaching an all-time high of $2,465 on May 25, 2017, after peaking at nearly $2,900. This sharp increase in value is believed to be the result of a strengthening demand for bitcoin in Japan.

On August 14, 2017, the price of Bitcoin surpassed the USD 4,000 mark.

On October 12, 2017, the rate crossed the symbolic USD 5,000 mark for the first time. It will then get carried away since, eleven days later, on October 23rd, it crossed the 6,000 USD mark. Eleven days later, on November 3, the USD 7,000 mark was crossed. Sixteen days later, on November 19, the USD 8,000 mark was reached. One week later, on November 26, Bitcoin broke the $9,000 mark, and $10,000 on November 30. By that time, it had doubled in value in a month and a half.

The increase is even more pronounced, with USD 11,000 crossed on December 2, 2017. The 12,000 and 13,000 USD are both crossed on December 5 and the 14,000, 15,000 and 16,000 USD are crossed the following day, December 6, for an increase of 5,000 USD and more than 40% in two days. The $17,000 is crossed on December 7. The

$18,000 is crossed on December 15 and the $19,000 is crossed the next day.

The price then falls drastically and on Friday December 22, Bitcoin is valued at USD 14,400 or EUR 11,800. It fell back below 13 000 USD at the end of the year.

Design

School of Economics

Bitcoin's theoretical roots lie in the Austrian school of economics and its critique of the current monetary system and the interventions of governments and other bodies, which, according to this school, exacerbate economic cycles and massive inflation.

One of the topics on which the Austrian School of Economics, led by Eugen von Böhm-Bawerk, Ludwig von Mises and Friedrich A. Hayek, has focused is the business cycle: according to Austrian theory, business cycles are the inevitable consequence of monetary interventions in the market, whereby excessive expansion of bank credit leads to an increase in the outstanding amount of bank credit in a fractional reserve system, which in turn leads to artificially low interest rates.

In this situation, entrepreneurs, guided by distorted interest rate signals, embark on overly ambitious investment projects that do not correspond to the intertemporal consumption preferences of consumers at that time . Sooner or later, this generalized imbalance can no longer be sustained and leads to a recession, during which firms have to liquidate failed investment projects and readjust their production structures according to consumers' intertemporal preferences. Consequently, many economists in Austrian schools are calling for the abandonment of this process by abolishing the fractional reserve banking system and returning to a currency based on the gold standard, which cannot be easily manipulated by any authority.

A related field in which Austrian economists have been very active is monetary theory. Friedrich A. Hayek is one of the best known names in this field. He wrote some very influential publications, such as *Denationalization of Money, in* which he postulates that governments should not have a monopoly on issuing money. Instead, he suggests that private banks should be allowed to issue non-interest-bearing certificates, based on their own trademarks. These certificates should be open to competition and would be traded at variable exchange rates. Any currency that can guarantee stable purchasing power would eliminate other, less stable currencies from the market. The result of this process of competition and profit maximization would be a highly efficient monetary system in which only stable currencies would coexist.

The following ideas are generally shared by Bitcoin supporters:

- they see Bitcoin as a good starting point to end the monopoly of central banks in issuing money ;
- they strongly criticize the current fractional reserve banking system, which allows banks to extend their credit supply beyond their actual reserves and, at the same time, allows depositors to withdraw their funds from their current accounts at any time ;
- The scheme is inspired by the old gold standard.

Specificity of Bitcoin

A distinction must be made between Bitcoin, the crypto-currency and on the other hand Bitcoin, the payment system in this currency. In these two aspects, Bitcoin differs from the pre-existing systems on the following points:

- Unlike other monetary currencies, Bitcoin is not the embodiment of the authority of a state, bank or company. The value of Bitcoin is determined in an entirely floating manner by the economic use made of it and by the foreign exchange market. The rules organizing the monetary issue are determined solely by the free computer code of the Bitcoin software;
- As a payment system, Bitcoin distinguishes itself by the fact that its operation does not require the use of a centralized infrastructure holding accounts of the amounts held in order to ensure transactions. The role of guarantee and verification exists, but is assigned approximately every ten minutes to a computer on the network randomly selected according to its power ;
- Bitcoin is based on a cryptographic protocol whose purpose is, on the one hand, to solve the so-called *double payment* problem, which until then had prevented the emergence of such a type of currency, and, on the other hand, to prohibit the falsification of the stakeholders' identifiers and the value of the stock of Bitcoins contained in electronic purses identified by a given address.

Monetary principle

From a monetary point of view, Bitcoin differs from other currencies by the major fact that the monetary aggregate is not designed to adapt to the production of wealth.

The total amount and the rate of emission of the units are written explicitly in the computer code of the software, according to a mathematical rule of geometric series type.

Bitcoins are emitted slowly and steadily, in a degressive manner, until they reach a maximum amount of 21 million around the year 2140.

All fiduciary currencies experience inflation, from low to high depending on the policies of their central bank. Conversely, Bitcoin currency is likely to eventually experience deflation, as the maximum amount of Bitcoins that can be created is set in advance in the software at 21 million. In addition, Bitcoins lost by users will never be replaced. This is why the Bitcoin project is seen by the community of its creators as an original experiment in economic terms, constituting a kind of test of the monetary theses of the Austrian School of Economics. Indeed, Friedrich Hayek, Nobel Prize winner in economics, had called in 1976 to restore monetary free will in his book *For a true competition of currencies*. The success or failure of Bitcoin is difficult to predict.

Scalability of the protocol

A limit of 1 MB per block to prevent malicious attacks

On July 14, 2010, shortly after the launch of the Bitcoin system, Satoshi Nakamoto created a limit of 1 MB for each newly created block every ten minutes on the Bitcoin block chain.

At that time, transactions were free because they were few in number, and developers had a legitimate concern that attackers could "spam" the transaction network, arbitrarily creating huge blocks and permanently inflating the size of the block chain. This limit was intended to prevent this kind of attack until a better solution could be put in place. Satoshi Nakamoto had proposed a solution that would involve increasing the block size at certain block heights, effectively increasing the limit at a predetermined rate and similar to the way new bitcoins are emitted.

The scalability of the Bitcoin system has since been a constant source of debate in the community since the introduction of this block size limit. This 1 MB limit, originally designed to limit the number of transactions per second to seven, was not a problem at a time when the actual number of transactions was only 2.3 transactions per second . Thus, seven transactions per second represented three times the volume of Bitcoin's most active day at that time, leaving developers years to find a better solution. In addition, the protocol called for the introduction of transaction fees over time, which would make these kinds of attacks more costly and inefficient.

Saturation of transaction integration capacity

Starting in 2014, the success of the Bitcoin system leads to a continuous increase in the number of transactions that eventually reaches the 1 MB limit in 2016. One developer, Gavin Andresen, initially proposed 20 MB blocks, but this increase was considered too aggressive by the community. Another proposal, BIP101, proposed to increase the block size by 40% per year from 8 MB, which led to the creation of a new crypto-currency, different from Bitcoin, called Bitcoin XT. Other proposals were made such as BIP100 with a 2 MB block size that led to the Bitcoin Classic crypto-currency and more aggressive "emerging consensus" approaches that allow users to "vote" the best block size at a given time through Bitcoin Unlimited. Other members of the community have preferred not to promote an increase in block size, but to change the protocol itself to allow more transactions to be embedded in a block by reducing their size or to increase the frequency of creating new blocks.

When the number of transactions finally reached the block size limit, the pool of transactions awaiting validation became saturated. The only way to get a given transaction into the block chain faster for a user was to increase transaction fees, which reached nearly $5 by the end of 2016. This made Bitcoin uncompetitive with existing services such as Western Union or Paypal on a strict speed and cost basis.

Compromise of the New York Agreement

The bogging down of the debate on scalability weakens the Bitcoin Core system and leads to the growing success of the vote in favor of the Bitcoin Unlimited movement, especially among miners, largely due to frustration with the lack of scalability solutions. The development team's approach, known as *segwit , of* not increasing the block size limit, but partitioning digital signatures of transactions differently into "extension blocks," failed to achieve sufficient consensus.

A compromise is reached in an industry consensus in 2017 called Segwit2x[,] which combines the *segregated witness* proposal with an increase in block size to 2 MB. This proposal is implemented on August [1,] 2017 for *segregated witness* and the increase in block size is implemented in November 2017 for block 494,784 and is a major upgrade of the Bitcoin Core system.

Nevertheless, the scalability debate is still lively and a splinter group unilaterally increased the block size to 8 MB while rejecting the *Segwit* proposal on August [1,] 2017. This decision led to the emergence of a new crypto-currency called Bitcoin Cash. The likelihood that another group may decide to implement *segregated witness* without increasing the block size in November 2017 may lead to the emergence of another crypto-currency, parallel to Bitcoin Cash and Bitcoin Core, whose blocks would be rejected after the Bitcoin Core protocol update.

Bitcoin XT , Bitcoin Unlimited , Bitcoin Classic , Bitcoin Cash and Bitcoin Gold are encryption alternatives to Bitcoin .

Distribution of wealth

Bitcoins are concentrated: the distribution of "wealth" is such that 2,100 addresses hold 40.2% of the total. However, this kind of information is not very useful because some of these addresses are dead.

How it works

Principle

Bitcoin does not exist independently of the Bitcoin payment system, which allows transactions to be made from one account to another, thanks to software called *wallets, the* authority being ensured by verification software called *minors*. The data of all transactions constitute a public register of private law called a *chain of blocks* because of its structure and an agent uses Bitcoins by recording in the chain of blocks of the Bitcoin system its transactions, said recording referring to previous transactions.

The Bitcoin system is computer-based, in other words, the Bitcoin system resides on the Internet. By downloading and installing the appropriate software, you can become a Bitcoin user by interacting with hardware of your choice, such as a smartphone or computer. In order to pay or be paid in Bitcoin, the user must log in to the system, which connection offers two functionalities: the creation of any number of accounts on the one hand, and on the other hand, the ease of carrying out transactions consisting of the transfer of Bitcoin from one's own account to the account of a third party.

The essential function of the Bitcoin system is that the transactions are subject to validity verification by the competent computers and are irrevocably registered in a public register. This public register or chain of blocks can be consulted anywhere, provided that one has a connection to Bitcoin, and by anyone. No alterations are possible during consultation. A Bitcoin transaction is carried out in two steps:

1. First, dedicated nodes in the network create a new block by grouping together recently completed transactions and attaching a header containing the date and time, a checksum that will also serve as the unique identifier of the block, and the identifier of the previous block;
2. In a second step, after checking the validity of all the transactions contained in this new block and their consistency with the transactions already recorded, each minor adds it to his or her local version of the registry .

The public register is copied in several copies. The complete history of all transactions can then be read by consulting all the nodes in the network that manage a copy of the block chain. The copy can show any differences between files in case of disagreement. In this case, any differences between these copies must be resolved by the access software.

Here are some of Bitcoin's features:

- its *functionalities* are implemented by software made available in the form of free software;
- the user *chooses* his role in the system and the software he uses;
- By design, the *trusted authority of the system is not central*, but distributed among the computers competent to build and maintain the block chain.

Transactions

Transactions consist of debiting some accounts and crediting others.

They are composed of inputs and outputs. Each output includes an amount and the public key of the credited address, or more generally a program to authorize or not to authorize the transfer of the amount of this output to another transaction. Each input designates an output from a previous transaction and includes a program that provides the data expected by the script in this output. The sum of the output values must be less than or equal to the sum of the input values, the difference constituting the remuneration of the minor.

When validating a transaction, the scripts for each input are executed; first the script for the input itself, then the script for the previous output to which the input refers. The transaction is validated only if the result is "true" for all inputs.

These scripts are written in an internal language designed by Nakamoto. This language is deliberately minimalist and not Turing-complete in order to avoid the system from engaging in infinite loops. The use of scripts should allow the software to easily adapt to future developments and support advanced features such as transactions involving multiple signatures or smart contracts.

Transactions made by a node are broadcast to its neighbors. The latter validate the transactions they receive and progressively group them in a local pool before transmitting them to their own neighbors. Valid transactions are then distributed to all the nodes in the network, after being checked again at each step.

Before definitively entering a transaction in the chain of blocks, the network performs a series of checks, including the fact that the outputs referenced by the entries do exist and have not yet been used, that the author of the transaction does indeed hold the address credited in these outputs, and that the sum of the amounts appearing in the outputs of the transaction is much less than or equal to the sum of the amounts of the outputs referenced by the entries.

The effect of entering a transaction in the block chain is to prohibit any future reference to the outputs designated by the inputs of that transaction, and thus to prevent a double expenditure of the amount of those outputs, which would amount to creating bitcoins ex nihilo in an unauthorized manner. The only authorized creation of bitcoin ex-nihilo is made by a special transaction called Coinbase inserted at the beginning of each block in the chain to remunerate the miner who inserted the block.

A transaction is taken into account instantly by the network and confirmed for the first time after about 10 minutes. Each new confirmation reinforces the validity of the transaction in the transaction log.

Addresses

Each user can have any number of addresses that he creates through his *wallet*. Each bitcoin address is associated with a public-private key pair.

An address is equal to the 160-bit cryptographic fingerprint of its public key. There are thus a maximum of 2^{160} possible bitcoin addresses, i.e. about 10^{48}. A bitcoin address also has a prefix identifying the version number and a checksum of four bytes. In all, a bitcoin address thus occupies 25 bytes.

An address is represented in ASCII format thanks to a dedicated coding on 58 alphanumeric characters: upper and lower case letters and numbers, with the exception of the letters and numbers l, I, 0 and O, which Nakamoto has excluded because of their similarity in some character fonts.

As an example, here is the very first bitcoin address that received bitcoins:
1A1zP1eP5QGefi2DMPTfTL5SLmv7DivfNa.

In order to use the sum contained in an output of an existing transaction crediting a Bitcoin address, the user must make use in the input of a transaction of the private key corresponding to the address by signing the transaction. The network verifies the validity of this signature using the public key associated with the credited address, using the techniques of asymmetric cryptography. The operation is repeated for each entry of the transaction.

Wallets

Each user's *wallet* contains their personal data, including the address, public key and private key of each of their accounts. It can also contain information specific to the user and built from the chain of blocks, such as the list of available transaction outputs or account balances.

The wallet software provides at least the functions of creating accounts, consulting accounts, building and sending transactions.

There is a choice of wallet software for all varieties of devices including smartphones. They differ in the scope of their ancillary functions and in their ergonomics.

The information contained in a user's wallet is critical and must be strictly protected against any intrusion.

If an account's private key is lost, the user can no longer access the transactions that fund that account, nor create new transactions from it. Its bitcoins are permanently lost and will remain forever in the database without being able to change address. In 2013, a user lost 7,500 Bitcoins, worth $7.5 million at the time, when he accidentally threw away the hard drive containing his private key.

The discovery of an account's private key by another user allows that user to impersonate the legitimate account holder and spend any Bitcoins that may be in the account, which amounts to theft of Bitcoins.

Mining

The mining operation consists of assembling transactions into "blocks", with a header indicating the size of the block, the number of transactions recorded, the date and time, a checksum prohibiting any modification of the block and also serving as a unique identifier of the block, as well as the identifier of the previous block.

Miners include in the blocks that they constitute a particular transaction that credits them with a number of bitcoins created for this purpose, and includes a specific transaction fee. This fee will only be effective, however, if the block is definitively accepted in the block chain by the other nodes. It is this creation of money that explains the use of the term "mining", by analogy with gold mining.

A block can contain any number of transactions, typically between 1,000 and 2,000, but the block size may not exceed 1 megabyte.

Within a block, transactions are stored in the form of a Merkle tree.

The checksum of the block is calculated by applying twice an SHA-256 hash to the constituted sixtuplet :

- the software version number ;
- of the header fingerprint of the previous block ;
- of the root of the transaction tree of the block ;
- time stamping ;
- difficulty ;

- of the nuncio.

The calculation of this fingerprint is intentionally made difficult by the requirement to be less than a certain value, which is materialized by a binary representation starting with a certain number of zeros. To this end, the fingerprint contains among its components, an arbitrary number of 32 bits, the "nonce".

Even if we know the fingerprints corresponding to certain nunces, the hash makes it impossible to determine the value of the fingerprint for a new nunce without running the algorithm again. Therefore, finding the appropriate nunce for the boundary requirement on the fingerprint value can only be done by making several attempts.

For a given nunce value, the probability of calculating a fingerprint below the difficulty is very low, so many attempts must be made before reaching it. Between 2014 and 2016, the average number of nunces that each miner had to test between each block creation increased from 1 billion to 200 billion. This calculation involves performing the same calculation a very large number of times using different data, so it lends itself well to parallel calculation.

The difficulty is readjusted every 2016 blocks to take into account the actual computing power of the network and to allow on average one block to be added every 10 minutes, which means that the probable computing time for a valid fingerprint is 10 minutes for the most powerful computer or group of computers on the network.

This system of proof of work and linking of blocks by their imprint makes any alteration of the chain of blocks practically impossible. An attacker who would like to modify a transaction in a given block would have to recalculate its checksum and that of all the following blocks. As the difficulty increases with time, as well as the number of blocks subsequent to the modified transaction, the time needed to make such a modification increases very quickly.

When a miner has constructed a valid block whose checksum satisfies the difficulty condition, he diffuses it to the neighboring nodes, which check its validity before replaying it in their turn. Remuneration for mining work is made in Bitcoin. The payment is known as a block reward. The current block reward is 6.25 Bitcoin. This reward is divided by two for every 210,000 blocks.

The valid blocks are thus distributed step by step to all the nodes of the network, not without having been checked beforehand, but can no longer be modified. From the nunce included in the header, it is easy and quick to check the validity of the block .

Power consumption

Although mining is often criticized for its allegedly high energy consumption, some observers weigh the criticism by pointing out that the "classic" money network consumes much more energy, through millions of cash dispensers or the infrastructure necessary for the proper functioning of the classic money system, such as data centers. The majority of bitcoin miners use renewable energy because it is cheaper in areas of the world conducive to mining.

Estimated power consumption

It is difficult to evaluate because of the decentralization of the activity. [The] figures most often cited by the press come from the "Digiconomist" site created by a Dutch financial analyst.

According to its estimate, which is based on the assumption of an economic balance between the revenues and costs of mining, the world's electricity consumption resulting from mining would be 71.1 TWh/year = 1 billion kilowatt-hours (1 billion kilowatt-hours) as of July 1, 2018, which is the energy produced for one year by six 1,300 MW nuclear reactors operating at full capacity, or Chile's annual electricity consumption, or 0.32% of the world's electricity consumption. Its growth is extremely strong, since it was estimated at only 13.7 TWh/year one year earlier, a multiplication by a little more than five times in one year.

With only about 200,000 transactions per day in 2018, Bitcoin's electricity consumption would be around 1,000 kWh per transaction as of July [1,] 2018. By way of comparison, Visa consumed 0.19 TWh/year to handle 111 billion transactions in 2017, or 0.001 7 kWh per transaction. Bitcoin would thus consume approximately 600,000 times more energy per transaction than Visa. It should be noted, however, that mining consumption is independent of the number of transactions.

The estimates of the "Digiconomist" site are nevertheless disputed and considered exaggerated. According to Marc Bevand, IT security engineer, they overestimate the electricity consumption of Bitcoin miners by a factor of 1.5 to 2.8, [which] would bring the total electricity consumption to 32.3 TWh/year, or 424 kWh per transaction.

These estimates are subject to uncertainty due to the assumptions they require, but it is possible to calculate a minimum power consumption for the Bitcoin network from verifiable data :

- the number of hashes per second: 37.1×10^{18} H/s on July [1,] 2018 ;
- the power and chopping capacity of the most powerful machine on the market: 1,323 W for 13.5×10^{12} H/s.

It can thus be stated that the Bitcoin network had at least 2.8 million mining machines on July [1,] 2018 and that its electricity consumption was at least equal to 32.2 TWh/year. The number of entities securing the Bitcoin network is constantly increasing, which increases the value of Bitcoin.

Why is power consumption so important?

Bitcoin's very high energy consumption is linked to the system of mining new blocks, as a proof of work supposed to protect the system from fraud in the absence of a central authority. Security is based on a mathematical problem that is difficult to solve and inherently expensive to solve. In order to have a chance of adding the next block to the chain, miners must invest heavily in server farms to have high computing power. These farms consume a lot of electricity to power and cool the servers.

In order to register a new block on the block chain, miners must solve a mathematical problem submitted to all those competing, and the first one to find a solution that proceeds to the registration and wins a bitcoin payment. Since the solution can only be found by trial and error, the miner who is able to do the maximum number of tries has the best chance of winning. The difficulty of the problem is adjusted so that the computing time required to solve it is of the order of 10 minutes.

The magnitude of the electricity consumption is related to the intensity of the calculations and the fact that these calculations are made simultaneously by a large number of miners. It is related to the price of Bitcoin, because the higher it is, the higher the pay increases and the more miners are involved, which brings to mind Henry Ford's prediction at the beginning of the 20th century: "An energy currency will replace gold and put an end to wars".

Grouping of minors

The difficulty of mining has led miners to form cooperatives to combine their computing resources and build new blocks faster. The remuneration corresponding to the constitution of each block is then divided proportionally among the members, after deduction of fees, thus smoothing their incomes and making them less uncertain. In 2016, about ten of these cooperatives will provide 95% of the blocks. Most of them are located in China, but also in the Czech Republic and Georgia.

Remuneration for mining activities has led to the development of increasingly specialized technologies. The most efficient hardware uses integrated circuits that outperform general-purpose processors while using less energy. As of 2015, a miner not using equipment specifically designed for mining had a low probability of covering his electricity and equipment costs, even by joining a mining cooperative.

Russia

A close associate of the Russian president wants to raise 100 million dollars to finance "mining" in order to compete with China.

Chain of blocks

The block chain of the Bitcoin system is comparable to a public book recording transactions. There are more than 10,000 copies of the block chain managed in parallel by the nodes in the network, none of which play a privileged role. Some copies of the register are stored in areas protected from cataclysm, such as in a bunker under the mountains in Switzerland, for example.

The operator of each node in the network may decide to install a "complete node" that builds and maintains a local copy of the block chain. Alternatively, the operator may choose to settle for a thin node that will use neighboring full nodes to validate transactions using the SPV protocol.

Since these decisions are totally decentralized, it is impossible to know the number of nodes of each type. The only population that is permanently counted by specialized sites such as *blockchain.info* or *bitnodes* is that of "listening" nodes that accept, at the time of measurement, transactions and blocks from other nodes. Their number is around 10,000.

The nodes in the network are likely to number in the tens of thousands. For complete nodes, corresponding to the number of copies of the block chain, estimates range from 5,000 to 30,000, located in 85 countries on all continents.

This redundancy ensures continuity of service. Each computer can disconnect or crash without jeopardizing the proper functioning of the entire system. When it becomes operational again, the protocol for building the chain of blocks it hosts automatically rebuilds the missing portion using neighboring nodes.

As long as he has access to the Internet, a user will always find a node in the network to accept and relay a writing, and then there will be a large number of minors and complete nodes, located all over the world, to write it down and make it accessible in the block chain, where it will always remain accessible from any point in the world that has access to the Internet, without being able to be modified.

This same redundancy, combined with the "precautionary principle" whereby each node on the network checks the validity of the information it receives before using it, makes it impossible for fraudulent entries to spread. Errors and frauds remain possible on a particular computer, whether they are made by the site operator or by a hacker who manipulates this site; it is even possible that they may spread locally by contagion or by connivance. On the other hand, it is virtually impossible for such pollution to spread to a significant percentage of the copies in the block chain, let alone to the entire network.

Construction of the block chain

Upon receiving a new block, each computer managing a complete node executes a protocol that results in either rejecting the block if it has already been received or if it is invalid, or adding it to the local block chain after a final check of all the entries it contains, or putting it on hold.

Each block contains the identifier of the block that precedes it in the block chain of its minor and, in the most common case, this predecessor is the terminal block of the local chain, to which the new block is added after a final check of its validity. The transactions contained in this new block are then validated by the node, in particular the one that pays in bitcoins the minor who created this block. This block is transmitted to neighboring nodes and, step by step, to the entire network. In case of failure when checking the validity of the block, it is kept on standby, and is incorporated into a secondary branch of the block chain.

If the node receives a new block that contains an entry already present in the local string, this block is rejected. It is therefore the first valid block received that each node will write in its block chain. Identical blocks built by other miners in the same 10-minute cycle will be rejected, so the miners will race to have their blocks added to the chain and be paid accordingly.

Due to the delay required for the blocks to propagate through the network, two blocks created in the same cycle may arrive in a different order depending on the receiving nodes, which then build different versions of the register. This is called a bifurcation . Most of the time, a bifurcation is temporary and the block chain construction protocol corrects it in the next cycle.

In order to ensure that all copies of the block chain are identical on all nodes, even though they are built independently, this protocol incorporates a so-called "consensus" mechanism, which is a central element of the system. The rule used by Bitcoin is to retain the chain whose construction of the blocks that make it up required the most work. To this end, the header of each block indicates the difficulty of the work that was done to build it. The fact that the checksum of the block respects the constraints imposed is the "proof of work" that guarantees that this work has been done.

If it appears, following the addition of a block to a secondary chain, that the secondary chain required more work than the main chain, this secondary chain must become the main branch. To do this, the program goes back to the point where it broke away from the main branch, revalidates one by one the blocks and the entries they contain, and adds each block to the end of the new chain under construction if these checks are satisfied, abandoning this process at the first error.

This very complex process is the real heart of the system, as it is the only way to modify the chain of blocks and its results are irreversible. It also provides functions such as solving bifurcation cases and rebuilding the chain in case of computer or network shutdown.

At the end of this second phase, each of the thousands of copies of the chain of blocks existing on the complete nodes was extended by a block chosen by each node from the miners' proposals by applying the programmed consensus rule. If all the complete nodes implement the same rules for the validation of entries and blocks, this additional block is the same for all the nodes, so that all the copies of the chain of blocks remain the same. A few thousand new entries are thus definitively recorded and become accessible on the thousands of corresponding sites.

Role of Cryptography

Cryptography is used to authenticate actors, but digital data is not encrypted: cryptography is only used to ensure the signature.

Signature keys

To be valid, each transaction must be signed, in the cryptographic sense of the term, using asymmetric cryptographic techniques. To this end, each Bitcoin address also constitutes the cryptographic fingerprint of a public key. Every transaction indicates as input the reference of a previous transaction justifying the availability of the funds subject to the transaction and as output one or more Bitcoin addresses and the amounts to be allocated to them. A transaction always balances its inputs and outputs.

In order to transmit bitcoins, a user must cryptographically sign a transaction referring in input to one or more previous transactions whose output amount is sufficient to cover the transaction. The private key used to sign this transaction must match the public key that has previously received Bitcoins. The user must therefore store all his private keys in a confidential and secure manner. The corresponding file in the software, called *wallet.dat,* must be kept and saved by the user in a confidential manner.

Cryptography enables the authentication and non-repudiation described above through transaction signing and one-way functions. At no time does the system ensure the confidentiality or encryption of data transmitted over the network. All transactions are therefore *unencrypted*.

Transactions are signed using elliptic curve cryptography, known as ECDSA. In this case, the curve used is *secp256k1.*

Transparency

Even if the software does not use any personal data of the user, anonymity is not guaranteed: a user's identity can be determined if he or she discovers it voluntarily, if his or her IP address is traceable, or possibly as a result of a meticulous and complex statistical study of the transaction database, or when the regulations of a state or group of states take legal measures to end the anonymity of transactions on virtual currency platforms. However, it is possible to remain anonymous on the Bitcoin network with certain so-called "mixing" services and a good knowledge of AML, KYC measures applied to the exchange platforms.

The Bitcoin system does not encrypt any of the data it uses. Cryptography is only used to create forgery-proof signatures and implement one-way functions. Only the private key portfolio can be encrypted by the user, but this is optional, is within the user's sole control and is not part of the system specifications: confidentiality may be the responsibility of the operating system or a suitable encryption software, as it is for any other file.

Proof of work

Bitcoin uses the proof-of-work method, originally devised to solve the problem of spam and implemented in the Hashcash system. The hashcash algorithms are SHA-256 and RIPEMD-160. A double hash in SHA-256 is used to obtain the block hash and thus the proof of work, while a SHA-256 followed by a RIPEMD-160 is used to construct the bitcoin addresses.

Monetary aspects

Units

The unit of account in the Bitcoin system is Bitcoin. The symbols used to represent it are BTC, XBT and " ". Bitcoin can also be subdivided into smaller units such as millibitcoin, microbitcoin or satoshi, which represents 10 nanobitcoins. The microbitcoin is sometimes referred to as a *bit*.

Following a proposed addition, the Unicode consortium agreed in November 2015 to add Bitcoin as one of its characters, assigning it the code 20BF.

Special features

As a virtual currency, Bitcoin has three particularities:

1. In terms of regulation, the lack of legal status and regulatory framework means that virtual currencies provide no guarantee of price or liquidity. The voluntary limitation of the number of units issued without indexation carries a risk of speculation leading to high volatility;
2. In terms of transparency, an encryption of the identities of beneficiaries and principals leads to total anonymity of transactions. The transactions carried out are recorded in a public register, but this traceability is limited: it does not make it possible to know the originator and the beneficial owner, it is neither certain nor systematic, it is neither technically nor legally exploitable;
3. In terms of extraterritoriality, the protagonists, the servers and the natural or legal persons who operate them may be located in countries and territories whose cooperation may be difficult to obtain.

The exchange terminals allow the exchange of Bitcoin virtual currency for legal tender, in the same way that an ATM allows you to withdraw cash from a bank. To do this, these terminals can take into account identification formalities based on biometric control: taking palm prints, scanning an ID card and comparing facial features with the photo that appears on their ID card.

Another particularity of Bitcoin is the irrevocability of an illicit transaction.

Proof of ownership

The user with Bitcoins can access them through a specific address and a password also called private key. Since knowledge of the private key is essential for signing transactions, Bitcoins cannot be spent without it. The network verifies the validity of the private key with the user's public key using asymmetric cryptographic techniques. However, only the knowledge of the public key of an address is necessary to make a deposit.

Transactions and fees

Transactions

Bitcoins from different transactions cannot be grouped together. A user receiving several payments will keep as many different amounts in his portfolio, even if his software, in order to make it easier to read, makes a global display. When the user wants to spend them, his software will calculate the best set of input data to transfer to minimize the size of the output data and thus limit transaction costs.

- *Example*: A user receives 13 payments of 1 × 2.3 XBT, 5 × 1.0 XBT, 2 × 0.7 XBT, 1 × 0.5 XBT, 1 × 0.3 XBT, 2 × 0.2 XBT, and 1 × 0.1 XBT. His software will then tell him that he has 10.0 XBT.
- When he wants to spend 3.0 XBT, the best set of output data will consist of combining the 2.3 XBT and 0.7 XBT previously received.
- If he wanted to spend 3.05 XBT, the best output set would be to combine the 2.3 XBT with the 0.7 XBT previously received and split the 0.1 XBT transaction into an output transaction of 0.05 XBT, with the other 0.05 XBT transaction fraction retained in the portfolio.

Fees

The payment of transaction fees is theoretically optional, but the miners determine the order of processing of transactions to be included in the new blocks based on the transaction fees offered by users. The more a user agrees to pay a high transaction fee, the faster their transaction will be processed. In case of identical fees, priority is given to the oldest transactions. Transactions with no transaction fee are processed after all others; in practice, these transactions start to be processed on average from 120 minutes and up to a potentially infinite amount of time.

The most competitive transaction fees, which allow an almost immediate confirmation, between 0 and 35 minutes on average, are around 80 satoshis/byte . Thus, in 2016, for a median transaction size of 265 bytes, this represents a cost of approximately 21,200 satoshis regardless of the amount of bitcoins to be transferred.

To discourage the multiplication of small amount transactions, the software applies a mandatory transaction fee of 0.000 1 XBT to any transaction under 0.01 XBT.

The larger the input data assemblages to complete a transaction, the longer it takes to encode it and the higher the costs, while still remaining very low overall. Bitcoin's algorithm is designed to avoid as much as possible the aggregation of input data below 0.01 XBT in order to limit mandatory transaction fees.

If the amount of bitcoins to be transferred is small or if the transaction is recent, only the payment of a transaction fee will allow immediate processing of the transaction. Each transaction is prioritized according to its amount, age and size, which in turn is determined by the number of entries that have been grouped together. More precisely, the software calculates a quotient determined by the number of bitcoins to be transferred multiplied by the age of the transaction and divided by the size of the grouped input data. Below a certain quotient, the transaction will only be processed immediately upon payment of a transaction fee.

- If the User chooses not to pay a transaction fee, the quotient will increase over time until it exceeds a threshold value that will trigger the transaction to be processed; the transaction will then be processed free of charge but with a delay.

- The higher the number of bitcoins to be transferred, the higher the quotient and the faster or free of charge the user will see his transaction processed.
- For the same amount of bitcoins to be transferred, transactions with a small amount of input data are processed faster than others.

Bitcoin software usually calculates the optimal fee to be paid for the transaction to be processed at the time of transfer. These fees vary depending on the number of transactions to be processed at the time of transfer, but overall they are very negligible. The user alone decides the amount of the transaction fee he is willing to pay.

Special cases

- If a user has 3 XBTs from two transactions of 1 and 2 XBTs in their portfolio and wishes to purchase a product or service costing 2.999 XBTs at *no charge*, Bitcoin software will need to combine the two transactions and split the 1 XBT transaction into one line of 0.999 XBT and one line of 0.001 XBT. But in this case, the 0.001 XBT line would be charged an automatic 0.0001 XBT fee. The user would then be unable to make his purchase which would cost him 2 XBT + 0.999 XBT + 0.0001 XBT while he owns 3 XBT and wishes to keep 0.001 XBT. In such a case, it would be preferable for him to send 3 XBT to the seller at no cost, even if some sellers wish to have the precise amount of the purchase sent to them.
- The site reddit reports the case of a user who won a jackpot of 1,280 XBT on a gambling site with a bet amount of 0.02 XBT. In order to transfer the jackpot amount, the gambling site had to collect 64,000 transactions amounting to 0.02 XBT in input data, which represented a transaction of 51,203 bytes; the

71

amount of the fee required for immediate processing was 0.026 XBT, or approximately €15, which is more than the amount of the player's bet, €12, or the fee usually paid for a normal transaction, €0.11, but much less than the amount of the winnings, €768,000).

- Some minors may choose to process transactions in violation of Bitcoin protocol rules. In this case, they include the transaction in a new block which they will manage to undermine in a longer time the lower their computing power is.

Creation of bitcoins

The creation of a new block is rewarded with bitcoins created for this purpose.

The amount of this award is halved every time 210,000 blocks of transactions are added to the block chain :

- From the creation of the first block until the 209,999th block, created on November 28, 2012, each miner was rewarded with 50 newly created bitcoins for the creation of a new valid block ;
- from Block 210,000 to Block 419,999, created on July 9, 2016, the reward was 25 Bitcoins for each newly created block ;
- from Block 420,000 to Block 629,999, created on May 11, 2020, the reward was 12.5 Bitcoins for each newly created block ;
- from block 630,000 to block 839,999, the reward is 6.25 bitcoins for each newly created block;
- etc

The next halving is expected to take place around May 2024, so the reward will increase to 3.125 bitcoins per block.

The reward system is tending towards zero as the 210,000 block series is completed, so that a maximum of 20,999,999.9769 bitcoins will *ultimately* be created, probably around the year 2140. The gradual decrease in the amount of new bitcoins rewarding the creation of new blocks will be offset by the development of transaction costs.

In other words, the inventor of the Bitcoin system sought to define a monetary policy whereby the number of Bitcoins could not exceed 21 million units in total, with the speed of creation of new units tending towards zero. Such a monetary system is called deflationary.

Privacy

The Bitcoin system indicates on the public register the amount of bitcoins associated with each address. All transactions recorded on the block chain are also public. The identity of the owners of Bitcoin addresses is not public, but can be determined, for example, by means of exchange platforms that register the identity of their users.

Trading platforms generally group their users' assets under a single address and re-allocate a bitcoin credit line to each of their users through their trading software. Users can then exchange their Bitcoins for other crypto-currencies or currencies. The platform secures its deposits by distributing them over several addresses or by storing them "cold" to prevent theft. When a user transfers his deposits from the platform to another address, the platform debits his credit line and transfers the amount to be exchanged from one of its addresses to the address indicated by the user.

Researchers at Stanford University and Concordia University have shown that, to prevent hacking, bitcoin trading platforms can prove their creditworthiness without revealing their addresses using zero-knowledge protocols.

Researchers have argued that without specific safeguards, Bitcoin payments are no more private than credit card payments.

Stock exchanges and financial instruments

Bitcoin, as a virtual currency is quite unclassifiable. Thus, some asset management companies consider that virtual money can neither be considered as a good father's investment, nor be compared to gold, because of the lack of income.

For SEC Chairman Jay Clayton, Initial Coin Offering is less protected than traditional securities, allowing more market manipulation and scams: For him, as with other investments, extreme caution and an awareness of the risk of losing everything is required.

No ICOs have been registered with the U.S. federal securities regulator, and the listing and trading of exchange-traded products that hold cryptography has not been approved by the SEC.

Market Platforms

Fiduciary currencies or crypto-currencies can be exchanged for Bitcoins through various exchanges or specialized exchange platforms active on the Internet, by making transfers by bank transfer. Brokerage fees are generally very low and users are required to provide proof of identity.

Escrow platforms connect buyers and sellers to exchange Bitcoins for cash, postal account money orders or bank transfers.

One-way points of sale make it possible to pay in Bitcoins, against payment of a fee, by debiting the corresponding amount in euros from bank cards or prepaid cards.

Finally, there are vending machines that generally charge a higher commission.

Since November 2016, the Swiss Federal Railways, in cooperation with SweePay, have been offering the purchase of Bitcoin from their train ticket machines, creating the world's largest Bitcoin distribution network.

Financiarization

Some brokers now offer the possibility to quote Bitcoin while some platforms offer the possibility to buy or sell crypto-money short or use leverage.

Complex financial instruments such as investment funds are developing.

The use of established financial intermediaries makes transactions more secure, as these operators are subject to strict regulatory rules; however, the volatility that characterizes bitcoin-based financial instruments can lead to losses as high as the profits that can be made.

Legal framework

The legal nature of Bitcoin is not a uniformly settled issue.

The international dimension of Bitcoin, in view of the regional character of the legal frameworks, rules out any global legal response, in the current state of the law.

In particular, the G20 considered that if cryptoactives raise issues with respect to consumer and investor protection, market integrity, tax evasion, money laundering and terrorist financing, then they should be managed by states rather than the G20 itself.

European Union

According to the European Central Bank, the extensive banking and financial regulation required of European Union member states does not apply to Bitcoin.

The European banking authority has warned consumers about the risks associated with Bitcoin, considering crypto-currencies as "virtual representations" of currency. It also recommended on July 4, 2014 to European banking and financial institutions not to use Bitcoin or offer services around it.

On October 22, 2015, the Court of Justice of the European Union confirmed that transactions exchanging Bitcoin for traditional currencies were exempt from VAT, considering Bitcoin to be a "virtual currency" and not a good or service.

Algeria

Algeria bans Bitcoin in Article 117 of the 2018 Finance Law.

Australia

In December 2013, the governor of Australia's central bank said, in an interview on the legality of Bitcoin, that "there would be nothing to stop people from deciding to make transactions in another currency in a store if they wanted to. There's no law against that, so we have competing currencies. »

Australia has officially confirmed that bitcoin will be treated as silver on July [1], 2017 and will no longer be subject to double taxation.

Belgium

The Minister of Finance indicated that government intervention with respect to the Bitcoin system does not appear to be necessary at this time.

The Central Bank of Belgium stated in a statement that "the threats to monetary stability posed by digital currencies issued by private actors are currently rather limited in their use as a medium of exchange, so their impact on financial conditions in the economy is small".

China

On December 5, 2013, the Chinese Central Bank banned local banks from trading in Bitcoin, a measure that caused a crash in the value of the virtual currency. BTC China, the world's leading Bitcoin transaction platform, prohibits users from making new Yuan deposits to their accounts "due to new government regulations". On January 8, 2014, the Chinese group Ali Baba banned payments in Bitcoin, in accordance with new Chinese regulations. A circular dated September 4, 2017 leads either to the closure of the exchange platform or to the end of acceptance of fiat currencies. In February 2018, the Chinese government announces that it intends to reinforce the ban by censorship of all Chinese or foreign Bitcoin exchange websites.

South Korea

Bitcoin and crypto-currencies are legal and recognized as financial instruments.

There are no restrictions on the possession and exchange of Bitcoin between individuals. Exchange platforms must ensure that they own at least 500 million Korean Won to protect traders and businesses from embezzlement and fraud.

The government of South Korea has agreements with 14 "virtual cash" exchange platforms, known as *currency exchanges, which* allow only those users whose identity is controlled by a financial player such as a bank to use these platforms.

The South Korean state also governs the following:

- prohibition for minors to exchange money ;
- tax on profits from the sale of bitcoins ;
- prohibition of ICO .

United States

Senator Tom Carper's parliamentary report provides an initial overview of Bitcoin's legal issues.

The report concludes that bitcoin is of economic interest and that its development should be regulated in order to contain its specific risks. Nor does it offer a firm legal definition of bitcoin.

On February 26, 2014, U.S. Senator Joe Manchin called for a ban on bitcoin in the United States because of its uncontrolled volatility and the risk that it could be used for illegal purposes, including money laundering. For the time being, the United States considers that virtual currencies developed on the Bitcoin model have no legal value but are assets that may be subject to taxation.

On December 10, 2017, the Chicago Stock Exchange institutionalized Bitcoin.

In 2018, authorities - including the Securities and Exchange Commission, and the Commodity Futures Trading Commission - prosecuted various players who carried out scams such as offering the prospect of making money with Bitcoin or binary options.

Indonesia

The Central Bank of Indonesia does not have a detailed policy to regulate or prohibit the use of bitcoin·

Japan

The Central Bank of Japan officially recognizes Bitcoin and Cryptocurrency as a means of payment).

Luxembourg

In February 2014, the Financial Sector Supervisory Commission issued a communication recognizing the status of Bitcoin and other crypto-currencies as a currency.

A first bank payment license was granted to SnapSwap by the Ministry of Finance in October 2015. The government has indicated that it actively supports the development of this technology.

Malaysia

The Central Bank of Malaysia issued a statement on January 3, 2014, stating that Bitcoin is not recognized as legal tender in Malaysia and that it will not regulate Bitcoin transactions, as users should be aware of the risks associated with the use of Bitcoin.

Morocco

On November 20, 2017, the Moroccan Foreign Exchange Office declared that transactions made via virtual currencies constitute an infringement of foreign exchange regulations, subject to sanctions and fines.

New Zealand

The Central Bank of New Zealand states: "Non-bank entities do not require central bank approval in schemes that involve the storage and/or transfer of value, so long as there is no issuance of circulating money.

The Netherlands

Cryptocurrencies such as Bitcoin are legal and provisions have been made to prevent money laundering through them.

Philippines

Cryptocurrencies have been legalized and trade is regulated by the Central Bank of the Philippines. The first two licenses were granted for local exchange platforms in August 2017.

United Kingdom

Bitcoin is considered "private money". When crypto-money is exchanged for pounds sterling or other fiduciary currencies, such as the euro or dollar, no VAT is due. However, VAT applies to all goods and services that could be exchanged for Bitcoins. Profits and losses made on crypto-currencies are subject to capital gains tax.

Russia

On February 6, 2014, Russia declares the currency illegal on its territory, arguing that the only official currency in Russia is the ruble and that no other currency can legally be used in the country. However, as of November 2016 it declared that it was "not illegal" according to the Federal Tax Service of Russia.

Singapore

In December 2013, the Monetary Authority of Singapore affirmed that trade in goods and services for Bitcoins constituted trade over which it was not within the authority's jurisdiction to intervene.

In January 2014, Singapore's Domestic Revenue Authority issued a set of tax guidelines under which Bitcoin transactions can be considered barter if they are used as a method of payment for real goods and services. Companies dealing in bitcoin trade will be taxed according to their sales levels.

Switzerland

In Switzerland, the Federal Council has considered Bitcoin to be a virtual currency of marginal use, and as such it is in principle subject to the legislation of regular currencies. However, it recommends that the authorities and the responsible consumer protection organizations call on Bitcoin users to exercise caution.

According to him, the execution of contracts concluded in virtual currencies can in principle be ensured and offences committed with these currencies are punishable.

For example, the professional trading of virtual currencies and the operation of trading platforms in Switzerland basically fall within the scope of the Money Laundering Act, which requires verification of the identity of the contracting party and identification of the beneficial owner.

However, from the Swiss point of view, there are no international standards regulating virtual currencies.

Thailand

On July 29, 2013, Thailand became the first country to ban the use of bitcoin on its territory after a decision by its Central Bank·

In 2016, the Central Bank of Thailand indicated that Bitcoin was not illegal but warned against its use.

Tunisia

The governor of the Central Bank of Tunisia Chedly Ayari affirmed his opposition to Bitcoin on April 5, 2016, because of its alleged risk for the financing of terrorism. His successor at the head of the Central Bank of Tunisia, Marouane Abassi, announced in April 2019 that Tunisia "is seriously studying the possibility of issuing a Bitcoin sovereign bond".

Vietnam

Cryptocurrencies such as Bitcoin are not regulated. In December 2016, the government confirmed the development of a legal framework that is expected to be completed by December 2017.

Relevance of the section

Bitcoin will always exist, whether it is prohibited or advised by the authorities, all you need to do is connect to the internet by cable or satellite to make a transaction in your ledger. In addition, people residing in countries hostile to Bitcoin can use a method such as those proposed by Samurai or Wasabi, for example, to avoid being traced.

Terrorism and National Security

Debate on terrorism

Various opinions have been raised regarding the real or alleged link between Bitcoin and terrorism.

On several occasions, Bitcoin has been presented as a tool that can be used for terrorist financing:

- in the United States, by Elizabeth Rosenber, former Treasury Counselor.
- in Belgium, by the Chairman of the Financial Information Processing Unit Philippe De Koster ;
- in Morocco, by Abdellatif Jouahri, Wali of Bank Al-Maghrib ;
- in Germany, by the CSU ;

These allegations linking Bitcoin and terrorism, however, have not been found by law enforcement, according to a Europol report from January 2016.

Alleged risks

From the very beginning, Bitcoin has been the subject of many discussions - technical, economic and even political.

From these discussions, a number of pros and cons were discussed. Some of these comments are not necessarily specific to Bitcoin and could be applied to other payment systems with similar characteristics.

Recently, however, it has become apparent that there is little or no understanding of the nature and extent of the risks associated with bitcoin.

Bitcoin, like most existing cryptosystems, has no subjective assets or guarantees. Whoever buys Bitcoin pays the seller exclusively. Consequently, the increase in the value of the currency comes exclusively from the continuous presence of a flow of buyers capable of supporting its price. On closer inspection, the functioning of Bitcoin is therefore much more similar to that of a pyramid system than to that of a monetary system.

Volatility

- Bitcoin is a volatile currency because the number of coins is limited in the face of growing demand.
- The course evolves according to the latest news on crypto-currencies.
- Cryptocurrency is floating like any other currency and fluctuates differently against different currencies.

Irreversibility
A bitcoin transaction is irreversible and cannot be reversed.
Security flaw in its technology or the way users use it

- Portfolios poorly protected by password.
- New features are under development to make currency more accessible.
- The technology is exposed to denial of service attacks and 51% attack.

Internet dependency
The Bitcoin protocol is an overlay of the IP protocol which is the basis of how the internet works. In the event of an Internet outage or if a government does not promote/defend Internet neutrality, the Bitcoin protocol could be slowed down or even completely blocked by Internet providers or a state. Unless the user is using one of Blockstream's satellites.

Technical limitations
Giganticism

- The size of the database has grown very quickly and requires several gigabytes of memory in a hard disk. Some experts have wondered about the future size of this database and are discussing possible solutions to save disk space such as pruning the oldest transactions that form the Merkle tree, although this does not seem necessary in view of the progress made in the field of storage.

- Increased bandwidth requirements to load all the blocks in the block chain.
- The size of the block: Bitcoin "super-nodes" are envisaged to facilitate the propagation of information through the nodes of the network, which are struggling to keep up with the increasing size of the database. Some experts argue that Moore's Law could help track network growth using personal computers.

Institutional risk

To convert crypto-money into foreign currency, it is often necessary to go through an exchange platform operated by private companies that are potentially vulnerable to failures or bankruptcies, as happened at Mt. Gox. However, it is possible to exchange your Bitcoins for cash, gold or a service to avoid this pitfall.

Environmental impacts and risks

They are related to the electricity consumption generated by mining, which represents an estimated 0.15% to 0.32% of the world's electricity consumption. They are low when the latter is produced from renewable energy sources, but significant for fossil fuels. More and more server farms are being installed in cold-climate countries with cheap renewable energy, such as Canada and Iceland.

A study on the origin of the electricity consumed by mining farms shows that 74.1% of the energy consumed is produced from renewable energy sources.

On the other hand, mining leads to a significant use of graphic cards and computer components containing rare and non-recyclable metals. Bitcoin thus contributed to the shortage of graphic cards at the end of 2020 and beginning of 2021.

Ethical Risks

Criticisms of Bitcoin's philosophy and its economic concept, in comparison with state currencies or the gold standard.

Bitcoin would favor the early buyers of the currency . This allegation is sometimes confirmed by some studies showing that the distribution of wealth in Bitcoin is very unequal, and sometimes disproved by others.

Fraud risks, systemic risks, and speculative risks

- It has been suggested that Bitcoin could be likened to a Ponzi scheme, but this is not applicable: the price of crypto-money is a balance between buyers looking to buy the currency and sellers looking to sell it. In a Ponzi scheme, the new entrants pay the old entrants.
- When the price of Bitcoin surpassed $1,200, some articles referred to the phenomenon as tulipomania.
- Charles Stross and Paul Krugman took a stand against Bitcoin.
- Bitcoin's technology has been hijacked by organized crime as the only means of payment on Silkroad.

Alleged benefits

Flexibility and versatility

With Bitcoin it is possible to send and receive money, converting it into virtual currency :

- all over the world;
- at any time, regardless of holidays ;
- almost instantaneously: transactions are very fast from a few seconds to a few hours;
- without limitation: unlike a bank that sets daily or monthly ceilings ;
- independent of the currency issuing policies of monetary authorities because the issuance of Bitcoins is described in the software source code and requires the approval of more than 50% of the computing power.

Security

- In principle, only the users are able to order the completion of a transaction.
- The transaction is irreversible, which is a protection for the seller, who cannot be repudiated by the buyer after shipping the goods or service.
- Merchants may not charge additional fees without prior notice to the purchaser.
- The crypto-money is elusive if it is sufficiently protected.
- The protocol is very difficult to be manipulated by an individual, an organization or a government because it is written in the source code of the software and requires that more than 50% of the entities that undermine the blocks accept these modifications.

Transactional transparency

- All finalized transactions are available and searchable by everyone on the public registry of the block chain.

- Anyone can check transactions at any time.
- Transactional transfers can be traced from address to address.

Safe haven value

- Bitcoin retains its value against currencies undergoing high inflation.

Wide distribution

The payment protocol has gradually gained a foothold with merchants and continues to grow rapidly.

Robustness

Despite several crises, crypto-money has proven to be resilient.

Relevance of the concept

The concept behind open virtual currencies is also being considered by banks, financial institutions and monetary authorities who could develop legally secure regulated virtual currencies.

Technology is of increasing interest to banks and official monetary authorities.

Criticism and opinions

Opinions

Economists have expressed various opinions on Bitcoin.

For the American Nobel Prize winner in economics Joseph Stiglitz, Bitcoin is a bubble that will be very exciting as long as it goes up before it comes down. For him, it serves no socially useful function. Its success is due to its ability to bypass. Because of this, he feels that Bitcoin should be banned.

The French Nobel Prize laureate in economics Jean Tirole warns that Bitcoin is "an asset without intrinsic value", "without economic reality". He is dubious according to two criteria: is it a viable currency in the long term? Does it contribute to the common good? As far as viability is concerned, Jean Tirole is particularly critical of the Initial coin offering of three billion dollars in 2017. Announced as an instrument of financial disintermediation, the ICOs neglect, according to him, the fundamentals of finance: the use of reliable and well-capitalized intermediaries to follow projects, which is not the case for some Bitcoin players who are surrounded by secrecy. For the economist, the social role of Bitcoin is "elusive". Bitcoins are concentrated in private hands for fraud in general and tax evasion in particular.

Bill Gates , Jack Dorsay , Richard Branson , Chamath Palihapitiy , the Winklevoss brothers and a series of other billionaires see Bitcoin as inevitable.

The American Nobel Prize for Economics Paul Krugman had already judged in 2013, in the *New York Times,* that "Bitcoin is Evil".

According to Randall Quarles of the US Central Bank, Bitcoin is not backed by secure assets, has no intrinsic value and is not issued by a regulated banking institution.

The economist Thomas S. Umlauft from the University of Vienna :

1. Denies Bitcoin the essential characteristics of a currency: Bitcoin, like other crypto-currencies, does not meet the requirements of the two ruling schools regarding the creation and nature of money - according to the orthodox school, an intrinsic value, or according to the heterodox school, a support by a state ;

2. Affirms that the high limit of 21 million Bitcoin is also intrinsically a factor preventing Bitcoin from becoming a currency, as no other currency has an upper limit;
3. Declares that the current value of Bitcoin is only due to a cognitive bias of investors, who consider that Bitcoin has a value, due to the investment required by the mining, while lacking intrinsic utility, the final value of these crypto-currencies can only tend towards zero.

Bitcoin would be a scam because of Pump and Dump

Bill Harris, former CEO of PayPal, says "Bitcoin is the biggest scam in history", criticizing in particular the phenomena of *pump and dump,* which consists of manipulating the price of a crypto-currency in a coordinated manner with a group of people in order to buy at low prices, raise the price, and resell at the highest. The rise being artificial, the value then returns to its initial price, and those who bought at the highest price lose money.

Ethereum

Ethereum is a decentralized exchange protocol allowing the creation by users of intelligent contracts thanks to a Turing-complete language. These intelligent contracts are based on a computer protocol allowing to verify or implement a mutual contract. They are deployed and publicly available in a blockchain.

Ethereum uses a unit of account called **Ether** as a means of payment for these contracts. Its corresponding acronym, used by the exchange platforms, is "ETH". Ethereum is the second largest decentralized cryptographic currency with a capitalization of more than 37 billion euros in November 2020.

In July 2016, Ethereum's development team had to make a hard fork after a successful attack by a group of hackers on an Ether investment fund called The DAO in which nearly 3,641,694 ETH were hijacked to an address not controlled by The DAO members. This hard fork made it possible to cancel the misappropriation and return the funds to the decentralized autonomous organization. Nevertheless, this change did not meet with an absolute consensus and a small part of the community did not implement this change which led to the formation of two separate chains of blocks: one official one with the monetary unit Ether and its spin-off with the monetary unit classic Ether .

History

Origin and launch

Programmer Vitalik Buterin discovers cryptomoney with Bitcoin in 2011 and decides to create a new protocol using a "Turing-Complete" language rather than making the structure of Bitcoin heavier, the idea of Ethereum was born. In December 2013, Vitalik Buterin publishes a description of his Ethereum project in the form of a white paper with the aim of launching decentralized applications. At the beginning of 2014, he puts the first Ethers on pre-sale to finance the development of the project. The sale enabled him to collect 31,591 bitcoins worth more than 18 million dollars at the time, for 60 million Ethers sold. The Ethereum block chain was launched on July 30, 2015, but originally Buterin did not seek to create a crypto-money.

The first version of the software, called *Frontier,* was developed by the Swiss company Ethereum Switzerland GmbH , then managed by Joseph Lubin. Another Swiss company, The Ethereum Foundation, a non-profit organization, was also created to promote the development of this new currency.

In March 2016, the new version of the software is named *Homestead.*

The next versions of *Metropolis* followed by *Serenity are under* development.

TheDAO and its hacking

In May 2016, a decentralized autonomous organization was created to raise funds, in the form of Ether, to finance projects using the Ethereum block chain. This creation was widely acclaimed by the community and its investors by gathering more than 12,000,000 ether before a loophole in *TheDAO's* code was exploited by hackers who diverted, on June 17, 2016, nearly a third of the funds raised by the project to move them into a clone in which, according to *TheDAO*'s own rules, the funds are frozen as a precautionary measure for a period of one month.

During this time, the Ethereum community and its founding members debated to decide on the best method to recover or not the diverted Ether and whether to liquidate *TheDAO*. They decided to liquidate the investment fund and reprogram the block chain to reverse the effects of the hacking and re-credit the investment fund with the stolen funds in order to eventually reimburse the investors.

However, about 15% of the computing power of the Ether miners refused to implement this change resulting in the creation of two separate block chains, one official and supported by the developers, and the other unofficial with the *classic* Ether currency in which hackers keep *TheDAO's* misappropriated currency. This new currency is thus dissociated and distinct from the Ether, constituting a new crypto-currency with low computing power making it potentially more vulnerable to a 51% attack.

Before the implementation of the block chain reprogramming, any address that had Ether was therefore duplicated with the same amount in ETH in the official block chain and the same amount in ETC in the outgoing block chain. The ETC, a new crypto-currency, can only be used on the block chain supported by the sedition miner network and the ETH can only be used on the official reprogrammed block chain. If a block chain is split in two, users may be potentially vulnerable to replay attacks in which an attacker intercepts a transaction on one of the chains and rebroadcasts it on the second. Since the user's private key is the same on both chains, the signature of the initial transaction will also be valid on both chains.

At the end of September 2016, the value of the classic Ether represented about 10% of the value of Ether on the exchanges that agreed to trade this new crypto-money, after an introduction at about 3% and a peak at more than 45% at the beginning of August 2016.

Decentralized collaborations

Ethereum allows the emergence of new modes of collaboration thanks to the reduction of transaction costs, in the economic sense of the term, between collaborators.

General characteristics

The very first block called *"genesis block"* is created on July 30, 2015. It distributes the 60 million Ethers from presales and 12 million Ethers to developers. Since then, the release of new Ethers has only been possible by *"mining"* the blocks, a process by which transactions are verified, recorded and secured in the *"blockchain"*. The software pays the miners 2 Ethers per mined block, i.e. on average every 13 seconds, which means that more than 5 million new Ethers are emitted per year.

It is planned to change the current *Proof-of-Work* mining process to a *Proof-of-Stake* mining process in 2018, in a later version of the software called *Serenity, in* order to limit the electricity consumption of the Ethereum network. This update will also include changes concerning the emission of Ethers. The miners' remuneration should probably decrease, but the issue has not yet been decided by the developers.

The Ether can be subdivided into several multiples and sub-multiples :

As for Bitcoin, Ethers can be stored in a wallet. This one is associated to a public key, as well as a private key.

Cost of executing smart contracts

The execution of a smart contract, whether it is a simple Ether transfer between two accounts or the execution of several lines of code in a contract, requires paying minors for the task performed. This remuneration is done in Ether on an infinitesimal scale and is then called gas. Each operation on the *Ethereum* block chain "costs" gas corresponding to the effort required to process this operation. The price of gas evolves according to the market: each miner can set his price and corresponds to the number of Ether he wishes to receive for the effort he provides.

In June 2016, the average gas price was 0.0000000225 Ether. Thus, a basic transfer transaction between two addresses requiring 21,000 gases corresponds to an average cost of 0.00047 Ether in processing fees. This system allows :

- poorly performing or stingy miners to refuse to deal quickly with overly heavy operations by demanding high gas prices ;
- to avoid that some contracts become overpriced when the price of ether appreciates; in fact the

number of gases necessary for the execution is defined by the complexity of the operations while the price of gas can be adjusted according to the ether price;

- prevent an infinite loop in a code from running forever because at the moment when all the gas supplied in the transaction has been consumed, the miner stops processing the transaction and cancels the transaction

The user chooses the price he is willing to pay: if he pays below the average price, the execution of his contract will take much longer since all the more remunerative transactions are executed in priority.

Ripple

Ripple is a real-time gross settlement system, foreign exchange market and remittance network by the Ripple Company. Also known as the Ripple *Transaction Protocol* or **Ripple protocol,** it is built on a distributed and open source internet protocol, a consensus registry and a native currency called **XRP** . Launched in 2012, the Ripple network aims to enable "secure, instantaneous and virtually free global financial transactions of any size without chargebacks. It supports any cash, crypto-currency, convenience or any other unit of value such as air miles, mobile minutes,... At its core, Ripple is based on a shared public database or registry, which uses a consensus process to enable payments, exchanges and remittances in a distributed process.

The network is decentralized and can work without Ripple, it cannot be closed. Validators include companies, Internet service providers and the Massachusetts Institute of Technology.

Used by companies such as UniCredit, UBS and Santander, the Ripple protocol is increasingly being adopted by banks and payment networks as a settlement infrastructure technology, with *American Banker* explaining that "from a bank's perspective, distributed registries like Ripple have a number of advantages over crypto-currency like bitcoin," including price and security.

History

Start of development

The predecessor of the Ripple payment protocol, Ripplepay, was developed in 2004 by Ryan Fugger a web developer in Vancouver, British Columbia. Fugger conceived the idea after working on a local exchange system in Vancouver. His intention was to create a monetary system that would be decentralized and could allow individuals and communities to create their own money efficiently. Fugger's first iteration of this system, RipplePay.com, debuted in 2005 as a financial service to provide secure payment options to members of an online community via a global network.

This led to the design of a new system by Jed McCaleb of the eDonkey network, which was designed and built by Arthur Britto and David Schwartz. In May 2011, they began developing a digital currency system in which transactions were verified by consensus among network members, rather than by the mining process used by bitcoin, which is based on block-chain registers. This new version of the Ripple system therefore aimed to eliminate the use of centralized Bitcoin exchanges, use less electricity than Bitcoin, and perform transactions much faster than Bitcoin. Chris Larsen, who had previously founded the loan services companies E-Loan and Prosper, joined the team in August 2012, and together McCaleb and Larsen approached Ryan Fugger with their digital currency idea. After discussions with long-time members of the Ripple community, Fugger handed over the reins. In September 2012, the team co-founded OpenCoin· or OpenCoin Inc.

OpenCoin and Ripple Labs

OpenCoin has started to develop a new payment protocol called the *Ripple Transaction Protocol* based on concepts from Ryan Fugger. The Ripple Transaction Protocol allows the direct and instant transfer of money between two parties. As such the protocol can bypass the fees and delays of the traditional correspondent banking system· and any type of currency can be exchanged including US dollars, euros, yuan, yen, gold, miles, and rupees. To maintain security OpenCoin has programmed Ripple to rely on a common registry that is "managed by a network of independent validation servers that constantly compare their transaction records. The servers could belong to anyone, including banks or market makers. The company has also created its own form of digital currency called XRP in a similar way to Bitcoin, using it to allow financial institutions to transfer money with negligible fees and waiting times.

Early investors in OpenCoin included Andreessen Horowitz and Google Ventures. On July 1· 2013, XRP Fund II, LLC was incorporated as a wholly owned subsidiary of OpenCoin, headquartered in South Carolina. The following day, Ripple announced its linking of the Bitcoin and Ripple protocols via the Bitcoin Bridge. The Bitcoin Bridge allows Ripple users to send a payment in any currency to a Bitcoin address. Ripple has also developed early partnerships with companies such as ZipZap. On September 26, 2013,

OpenCoin Inc. changed its name to Ripple Labs Inc, with Chris Larsen remaining General Manager. On the same day Ripple's client and server reference implementation became free software, released as open source under the terms of the ISC license. Ripple Labs continued as the main code contributor to the consensus verification system behind Ripple, which can "integrate with existing bank networks. In October 2013, Ripple continued on a more advanced partnership with ZipZap, the relationship being called a threat to Western Union in the press.

Focus on the banking market

In 2014, Ripple Labs has been involved in several development projects related to the protocol, for example making available an iOS client application for iPhone allowing iPhone users to send and receive any currency via their phones,,·. This Ripple client application no longer exists. In July 2014, Ripple Labs proposed Codius, a project to develop a new intelligent contract system that is "programming language agnostic".

Since 2013, the protocol has been adopted by a growing number of financial institutions as an "alternative remittance option" for consumers. Ripple enables cross-border payments for personal customers, businesses, banks, and Larsen was quoted as saying that "Ripple simplifies the process by creating transparent, point-to-point transfers in which banks do not have to pay correspondent banking fees. The first bank to use Ripple was Fidor Bank in Munich, which announced the partnership in early 2014. Fidor is an exclusively online bank based in Germany. In September of the same year, Cross River Bank based in New Jersey and CBW Bank based in Kansas announced that they would use the Ripple protocol. In December 2014 Ripple Labs began working with Earthport's global payment service, combining Ripple software with Earthport's payment services system. Earthport's customers include banks such as Bank of

America and HSBC, Earthport operates in 65 countries. The partnership marked the first network use of the Ripple protocol. In December 2014 alone, the XRP value increased by over 200%, helping Ripple surpass litecoin to become the second largest crypto-currency, and bringing Ripple's market capitalization to nearly half a billion USD.

In February 2015, Fidor Bank announced that it would use the Ripple protocol to implement a new international real-time money transfer network, and at the end of April 2015, it was announced that Western Union intended to experiment with Ripple. At the end of May 2015, Commonwealth Bank of Australia announced that it would experiment with Ripple for interbank transfers. Since 2012, representatives of Ripple Labs have professed support for government regulation of the crypto-currency market, claiming that the regulations help businesses grow. On May 5, 2015 FinCEN fined Ripple Labs and XRP II $700,000 for violating the Banking Secrecy Act, based on the Financial Crimes Enforcement Network's additions to the law in 2013. Ripple Labs then agrees to corrective measures to ensure future compliance, which include an agreement to allow XRP exchange and Ripple Trade activity only by registered money service businesses, among other agreements was the enhancement of the Ripple protocol. The enhancement will not change the protocol itself, but instead will add anti-money laundering monitoring of network transactions and improve transaction analysis. In 2017, the current version of the server is 0.70.1.

2015 and 2016 marked Ripple's expansion with the opening of offices in Sydney, Australia in April 2015, followed by European offices in London, UK in March 2016 and Luxembourg in June 2016. Numerous companies have subsequently announced trials and integrations with Ripple.

On June 13, 2016, Ripple received a virtual currency license from the New York State Department of Financial Services, becoming the fourth company with a "BitLicense".

On August 19, 2016, SBI Ripple Asia announces the establishment of a Japanese banking consortium in a new network using Ripple's payment and settlement technology. The consortium is officially launched on October 25, 2016 with 42 member banks. As of July 2017, 61 Japanese banks had joined, representing more than 80% of total banking assets in Japan.

On September 23, 2016, Ripple announces the creation of the first interbank group for global payments based on distributed financial technology. As of April 2017, the members of the network known as the Global Payments Steering Group are Bank of America Merrill Lynch, Canadian Imperial Bank of Commerce, Mitsubishi UFJ Financial Group, Royal Bank of Canada, Santander, Standard Chartered, UniCredit and Westpac Banking Corporation. The group "will oversee the creation and maintenance of Ripple payment transaction rules, formalized standards for the Ripple business, and other actions to support the implementation of Ripple payment capabilities.

On October 10, 2017, Ripple announces partnerships with approximately 100 financial institutions. These banks or payment service providers will now use Ripple technology to provide their customers with an instant global payment service.

Concept

The Ripple website describes the open source protocol as "core infrastructure technology for interbank transactions - a neutral tool for financial institutions and systems. The protocol allows banks and non-bank financial services companies to integrate the Ripple protocol into their own systems, thereby enabling their customers to use the service. Currently, Ripple requires two parties for a transaction to occur: first, a regulated financial institution "holds funds and issues balances on behalf of customers. Second, "market makers," such as hedge funds or currency exchanges, provide liquidity in the currency they want to trade. At its core, Ripple relies on a shared public database or registry that has its contents decided by consensus. In addition to balances, the registry contains information about bids and offers to buy or sell currencies and assets, creating the first distributed exchange. The consensus process allows for payments, exchanges and remittances in a distributed process. According to CGAP in 2015, "Ripple does for payments what SMTP has done for e-mail, which is to allow the systems of different financial institutions to communicate directly.

In Ripple, users make payments to each other using signed cryptographic transactions, either in cash or Ripple's internal currency. For transactions denominated in XRP, Ripple can make use of its internal registry, while for payments denominated in other assets, the Ripple registry only records the amounts due, with the assets represented as debt securities. Since Ripple originally kept records only in its registry and has no real-world enforcement power, trust was necessary. However, Ripple is now integrated with various user verification protocols and banking services. Users need to specify which other users they trust and for what amount. When a non-XRP payment is made between two users who trust each other, the mutual credit line balance is adjusted, within the limits set by each user. To send assets between users who have not directly established a trust relationship, the system tries to find a path between the two users so that each link in the path is between two users who have a trust relationship. All balances along the path are then adjusted simultaneously and atomically. This mechanism making payments through a network of trusted partners is called "*rippling*". It has similarities with the age-old Hawala system.

Design Features

Gateways

A Gateway is any person or organization that allows users to put in and withdraw money from Ripple's liquidity pool. A gateway accepts users' foreign currency deposits and issues balances in Ripple's distributed registry. In addition, gateways refund the registry balances against the deposits they hold when the money is withdrawn. In practice, gateways are similar to banks, but they share a global registry known as the Ripple protocol. Depending on the type and degree of interaction between a user and a gateway, the gateway may have anti-money laundering or KYC rules requiring verification of identity, address, nationality, etc. These policies are designed to prevent criminal activity. Popular gateways in 2017 include Bitstamp, Gatehub, Ripple Fox, Tokyo JPY, Mr. Ripple, RippleChina and The Rock Trading.

Lines of trust and *rippling*

Users must "extend trust" to the Ripple Gateway that holds their repository. This manual creation of a trust line tells the Ripple network that the user is comfortable with the gateway's counterparty risk. In addition, the user must set a quantitative limit to this trust and create a similar limit for each currency on deposit at this gateway. For example, if a user deposits $50.00 and 2.00 BTC on Rock Trading, the user will have to trust the gateway with at least the same amount in both currencies in order for the funds to be available in the Ripple network. When a user has authorized multiple gateways in the same currency, there is an advanced option to allow "*rippling*", which subjects the user's balance in that currency to switch between the gateways. Although their total balance does not change, users earn a small transit fee to provide inter-gateway liquidity.

Solvency

For the same reasons as during the era of free banking in the United States, the value of a currency can vary significantly depending on the creditworthiness of a gateway. A non-profit trade association, the International Ripple Business Association, provides unified procedures and disclosure standards for gateways,". As of June 2015, fifteen companies have met or exceeded IRBA standards".

Consensus Registry

Ripple is based on a shared common registry, which is a database storing information about all Ripple accounts. The network is "managed by a network of independent validation servers that constantly compare their transaction records. The servers could be owned by anyone, including banks or market makers. Although it is free software, Ripple Labs continues to develop and promote the Ripple protocol that confirms financial transactions through a network of distributed servers. Ripple Labs is currently assisting banks in integrating with the Ripple network. A new registry is created every few seconds, and the last closed registry is a perfect record of all Ripple accounts as determined by the network of servers. A transaction is any change proposed to the registry and can be introduced by any server on the network. The servers attempt to reach consensus on a series of transactions to be applied to the registry, creating a new "last closed registry".

The consensus process is distributed, and the goal of the consensus is for each server to apply the same set of transactions to the current registry. Servers continually receive transactions from other servers on the network, and a server determines which transactions to apply based on whether a transaction comes from a node specified in the "Single Node List" or UNL . Transactions that are approved by a "qualified majority" of peers are considered validated. If the qualified majority is not in the consensus, "it implies that the volume of transactions was too high or the network latency too great for the consensus process to produce consistent proposals," and then the consensus process is again attempted by the nodes. Each round of consensus reduces disagreement until a qualified majority is reached. The expected result of this process is that disputed transactions are ignored from the proposals while widely accepted transactions are included. While users can assemble their own UNL nodes and have full control over which nodes they trust, Ripple Labs recognizes that most people will use the default UNL provided by their client.

Registry security

In early 2014, a rival company called the Stellar Foundation experienced a network failure. The company asked David Mazieres, Stellar's scientific director and head of the Secure Computing Group at Stanford University, to conduct a review of Stellar's consensus system, which was similar to Ripple's. The company was unable to find a solution. Mazieres said the Stellar system was unlikely to be secure when used with "more than one validation node," arguing that when consensus is not reached, a registry bifurcation occurs with parts of the network disagreeing on which transactions are accepted. The Stellar Foundation went on to argue that there was an "innate weakness" in the consensus process, an assertion that, according to *Finance Magnates,* "Ripple vehemently denied. Ripple's chief cryptographer David Schwartz challenged Mazieres' findings and declared Stellar's implementation of the consensus system flawed, noting that "the protocol provides security and fault tolerance assuming the validators are configured correctly". The company also wrote that, after reviewing Stellar's information, it had concluded that "there is no threat to the continued operation of the Ripple network.

Use as a payment/forex system

Ripple allows users or businesses to perform cross-currency transactions in 3-5 seconds. All accounts and transactions are secured by encryption and algorithmically verified. Payments can only be authorized by the account holder and all payments are processed automatically without third parties or intermediaries. Ripple validates accounts and balances instantly for payment transmission and provides payment notification with very little latency. Payments are irreversible, and there are no chargebacks. XRPs cannot be frozen or captured. While in 2014 anyone could open an account on Ripple, in 2015 identity verification procedures were implemented. Ripple's orientation algorithm searches for the fastest and cheapest path between two currencies. In the case of a user who wants to send a payment from USD to EUR, this could be a "one hop" path directly from USD to EUR, or it could be a multi-hop path, perhaps from USD to CAD to XRP to EUR. The routing algorithm is designed to look for the best conversion cost for the user. As of May 14, 2014, Ripple gateways allow deposits in a limited number of cash currencies, a handful of crypto-currencies and some raw materials".

The Bitcoin Bridge

The Bitcoin Bridge is a link between the Ripple and Bitcoin ecosystems. The bridge allows any Bitcoin user to pay directly from a Ripple account without ever having to own the digital currency. In addition, any merchant that accepts Bitcoin now has the potential to accept any currency in the world. For example, a Ripple user may prefer to keep an amount in US dollars and not own Bitcoin. However, a merchant may wish to accept payment in Bitcoin. The Bitcoin Bridge allows any Ripple user to send Bitcoins without having to use a clearing house like BTC-e to acquire them. Bitstamp acts as a gateway for the Ripple payment protocol, among other exchanges.

Privacy Policy

Although the transaction information on the registry is public, the payment information is not. This makes it difficult for anyone to associate transaction information with a specific user or company.

The market facilitators

Any Ripple user can act as a market maker by offering an arbitrage service such as providing liquidity to the market, intra-gateway currency conversion, *rippling,* etc. Market makers can also be hedge funds or currency exchange offices. According to the Ripple site, "by maintaining balances in multiple currencies and connecting to multiple gateways, market makers facilitate payments between users where no direct trust exists, thus enabling trading through the gateways. With a sufficient number of market makers, the referral algorithm creates a nearly frictionless market and allows payments between users seamlessly over the network in different currencies, without assuming any undesirable foreign exchange risk.

Many of these services are offered through a traditional bidding platform to buy or sell one currency against another currency. The bid and ask prices are grouped together in an order book to create a decentralized exchange. Users can trade with market makers to exchange or convert currencies. Ripple's referral algorithm exploits this functionality by allowing users to send money in one currency and recipients to receive it in another currency. For example, a user can pay in USD and the recipient can choose to receive the amount in another currency, including Bitcoins and XRP.

Open programming interface

Ripple Labs built the protocol to be easily accessible to the developer community, and the resulting features include an API for its payment network, based on the well-known REST standard. One of the first extensions by third-party developers was a Ripple extension to the Magento e-commerce platform, which allows Magento to consult Ripple's public registry and create an invoice. There was also a Ripple portfolio payment option developed for retail situations.

XRP

XRP is the native currency of the Ripple network which exists only in the Ripple system. XRP is currently divisible to 6 decimal places, and the smallest unit is called a drop with 1 million drops equivalent to 1 XRP. 100 billion XRPs were created during the genesis of Ripple, none of them can be created anymore according to the rules of the protocol. As such, the system has been designed so that XRP is a rare asset with decreasing quantity available. Not dependent on a third party for exchange, XRP is the only currency in the Ripple network that does not carry counterparty risk and is the only native digital asset. The other currencies in the Ripple network are debt instruments, and exist in the form of balances. Users of the Ripple Network are not required to use XRP as a store of value or a medium of exchange. Each Ripple account does, however, require a small reserve of 20 XRP. The purpose of this requirement is discussed in the anti-spam section.

Distribution

Out of the 100 billion created, 20 billion XRP were retained by the creators, who were also the founders of Ripple Labs. The creators donated the remaining 80% of the total to Ripple Labs, the XRPs being intended to "encourage market makers to increase XRP liquidity and strengthen the overall health of the XRP markets". Ripple Labs also had a short-term distribution program in 2013 of less than 200 million XRPs with some of the amount donated to charities such as Computing for Good initiative, which began offering XRPs in exchange for voluntary time on research projects. As of March 2015, 67% of the original 80% owned by Ripple Labs was still withheld by the company, with Ripple Labs stating that "we will engage in distribution strategies that we expect to result in a stable or strengthening XRP exchange rate against other currencies. In May 2017, to address concerns regarding the XRP offering, Ripple committed to place XRP 55 billion in cryptographically secure escrow. This will allow them to use up to 1 billion monthly and return anything not used each month at the end of the escrow in the form of an additional month's contract, starting the process all over again. The amount of XRP distributed and their movement can be traced through the Ripple Charts site.

As a monetary bridge

One of the specific functions of XRPs is as a currency bridge, which may be necessary if no direct exchange is available between two currencies at a particular time, for example when trading between two rarely traded currency pairs. In the network exchange office, XRPs are traded freely against other currencies, and their market price fluctuates against dollars, euros, yen, bitcoin, etc. Ripple's design focus is on the exchange office and distributed RTGS, as opposed to focusing on XRP as an alternative currency. In April 2015, Ripple Labs announced that a new feature called "*autobridging*" had been added to Ripple, with the intention of making it easier for market makers to trade between rarely traded currency pairs. The feature is also intended to increase the network's exposure to liquidity and better exchange rates.

As an anti-spam measure

When a user performs a financial transaction in a non-native currency, Ripple charges a transaction fee. The purpose of the transaction fee is to protect against network flooding attacks by making the attacks too expensive for hackers. If Ripple were completely open access, opponents could spread large amounts of "spam registry" and spam transactions in an attempt to overload the network. This could result in an unmanageable increase in the size of the registry and interfere with the network's ability to quickly settle legitimate transactions. Thus, to engage in an exchange, each Ripple account requires a small reserve of 20 XRP, and a transaction fee starting at 0.00001 XRP must be spent for each transaction. This transaction fee is not collected by anyone; the XRPs are destroyed and cease to exist. The transaction fee increases if the user posts orders at a huge rate, and recovers after a period of inactivity.

Reception

Since its inception, the Ripple Protocol has received a great deal of attention from both the financial press and the general public. Ripple has recently been mentioned in industry articles by Nielsen, the Bank of England Quarterly Bulletin, NACHA, and KPMG, with numerous articles examining Ripple's effect on the internationalization of the banking industry. In April 2015, *American Banker* stated that "from the banks' perspective, distributed registries like Ripple have a number of advantages over crypto-currencies like Bitcoin," including security. The *Federal Reserve Bank of Boston* wrote, "The adoption of distributed networks, such as Ripple, can help the industry achieve faster processing, as well as efficiencies for international payments and correspondent banking. Writing for *Esquire* on Ripple as a payment network in 2013, Ken Kurson stated that "the major financial services companies need to see Ripple the way the record companies saw Napster. The *New York Times*, Dealbook website noted in 2014 that "is gaining something that has so far proved elusive for virtual currencies: the involvement of several major players in the financial system. In August 2015, Ripple was recognized as a technology pioneer by the World Economic Forum.

Competitive Comparisons

Although Ripple is third in size to Bitcoin as a digital currency, many members of the press have described Ripple as a ready rival to Bitcoin. At the end of 2014, *Bloomberg* called Bitcoin a "failed" digital currency, after Bitcoin fell 54% in value in one year. Ripple has been described as an important competitor, in part because of its ability to transfer international money in real time. Bill Gates supports this perspective and mentioned the Ripple system when asked about Bitcoin in 2014, he said, "Bitcoin or Ripple and other variants can do a lot to make money transfer between countries easier and lower costs quite dramatically. But Bitcoin will not be the dominant system. On the compatibility of Ripple with any electronic value medium, St. Louis Federal Reserve Vice President and Simon Fraser University professor David Andolfatto said in 2014 that "Ripple is an agnostic currency protocol. Ripple is the winner. He can handle anything. For its creation and development of the Ripple protocol and the Ripple payment/exchange network, the Massachusetts Institute of Technology recognized Ripple Labs as one of the 50 Smartest Companies of 2014 in the February 2014 edition of the *MIT Technology Review*.

Reactions to XRP

Reaction to XRP is polarized in the crypto-currency community. Bitcoin proponents have criticized XRPs for being "pre-mined", since XRPs are directly integrated within the Ripple protocol and do not require mining. In addition, the distribution by Ripple Labs of a limited initial amount of XRP currency has generated a fair amount of controversy, and in particular the 20% withholding by the founders is considered a high percentage. However, *Esquire* countered the argument in 2013 explaining that "if this is deviant, then so is any company that has ever gone public while retaining most of its shares". Much of the controversy was settled after the announcement that founders Jed McCaleb and Arthur Britto would sell their XRPs at a mediation rate over several years, "a move that should increase stability and restore confidence in the XRP market. CEO Chris Larsen in turn donated XRP 7 billion to the Ripple Foundation for Financial Innovation, with XRPs being "locked up" and donated over time. By 2016, of the 20% initially allocated to the founders, nearly half had been donated to non-profit and charitable organizations,,.

Tether

Tether is a crypto-currency, stablecoin type, issued by the company Tether Limited·. Historically, the company claimed that each corner was backed by a U.S. dollar, but as of March 14, 2019, it changed its backing to include loans to affiliated companies,· In April 2019, the Attorney General of the State of New York accused the Bitfinex trading platform of using Tether to mask the absence of $850 million since mid-2018···. It is for these different points that Tether is controversial.

Tether is perceived as a stablecoin because it was originally designed to be worth $1.00 forever, retaining $1.00 in reserves for every Tether issued. Nevertheless, Tether Limited declares that the holders of Tether have no contractual rights, no other legal recourse, and no warranty other than the Tethers that will be exchanged. On April 30, 2019, counsel for Tether Limited asserted that each Tether was only protected to the extent of $0.74·.

Tether Limited and the Tether crypto-currency are controversial because of the company's inability to provide an audit showing sufficient reserves· because of its alleged role in manipulating the price of bitcoin, because of its unclear relationship with the Bitfinex platform, and because of the apparent lack of a long-term banking relationship. David Gerard writes in the Wall Street Journal, that the Tether is somehow the central bank of crypto trading, yet they do not conduct themselves as a responsible and sensible financial institution. The price of Tether, due to the loss of investor confidence in the area, dropped on October 15, 2018 to $0.90, its lowest level. On November 20, 2018, Bloomberg reported that U.S. federal prosecutors were investigating the use of Tether to manipulate the price of Bitcoin. In 2019, Tether outperformed Bitcoin in terms of daily trading volume.

History

In January 2012 JR Willett describes, in a white paper, the possibility to create new currencies in addition to the Bitcoin protocol. Willett helps to implement this idea in the *Mastercoin* crypto-currency, with which a *Mastercoin Foundation* is associated to promote the use of this new "second layer". The Mastercoin protocol becomes the basis of Tether, and Brock Pierce, one of the original members of the Mastercoin Foundation, becomes a co-founder of Tether. Another Tether founder, Craig Sellars, was the Technical Director of the Mastercoin Foundation.

Tether's ancestor, originally called "Realcoin", was announced in July 2014 by co-founders Brock Pierce, Reeve Collins and Craig Sellars as a startup based in Santa Monica. The first wedges were issued on October 6, 2014 on the Bitcoin blockchain using the Omni Layer protocol. On November 20, 2014, the management of Tether, through Reeve Collins, announced the new name of the project: "Tether". The company also announces that it is entering the private beta, which supports a "Tether + token" for three currencies: USTether for US dollars, EuroTether for Euros and YenTether for Japanese yen. The company states: "Each Tether + token is 100% guaranteed by its original currency and can be used at any time without currency risk." The company's website states that it is based in Hong Kong with offices in Switzerland, without giving details.

In January 2015, Bitfinex, a crypto-trading platform, integrates Tether on their platform. While representatives of Tether and Bitfinex claim that the two are separate, in November 2017, Paradise Papers unveiled the heads of Bitfinex, Philip Potter and Giancarlo Devasini, who established *Tether Holdings Limited in the* British Virgin Islands in 2014. A spokesman for Bitfinex and Tether said that the managing director of both companies was Jan Ludovicus van der Velde. According to the Hong Kong-based Tether website, *Tether Limited* is a wholly owned subsidiary of *Tether Holdings Limited*. Bitfinex is one of Bitcoin's largest trading platforms by volume in the world.

For a time, Tether processed U.S. dollar transactions through Taiwanese banks, which in turn sent the money through Wells Fargo Bank to allow the funds to flow out of Taiwan. Tether announced that on April 18, 2017, these international transfers were blocked. Bitfinex and Tether filed a lawsuit against Wells Fargo in federal court in the Northern District of California. The lawsuit was withdrawn a week later. In June 2017, the Omni Foundation and Charlie Lee announced that Tether would soon be published on the Omni layer of Litecoin. In September 2017, Tether announced that it would launch new ERC-20 tokens in U.S. dollars and Euros on the Ethereum block. Tether subsequently confirmed that the Ethereum tokens had been issued. Currently, there are a total of four separate tokens for attachment: the US dollar attachment on the Bitcoin Omni layer, the Euro attachment on the Bitcoin Omni layer, the US dollar attachment as the ERC-20 token and the Euro as the ERC-20 token.

From January 2017 to September 2018, the outstanding home linkages increased from approximately US$10 million to approximately US$2.8 billion. At the beginning of 2018, Tether accounted for approximately 10% of Bitcoin's transaction volume, but by the summer of 2018, it accounted for up to 80% of Bitcoin's volume. Research suggests that a price manipulation system involving tether accounted for about half of the increase in Bitcoin prices by the end of 2017. More than $500 million of Tether was issued in August 2018.

On October 15, 2018, the price of the lanyard dropped briefly to USD 0.88 due to perceived credit risk, as Bitfinex traders traded their emotions for Bitcoin, resulting in a rise in the price of Bitcoin.

Tether Limited has never substantiated their claim of full-backing through a promised audit of their currency reserves·.

In April 2019, New York State Attorney General Letitia James filed a lawsuit accusing Bitfinex of using Tether's reserves to cover an $850 million loss. Bitfinex failed to obtain a normal banking relationship under the lawsuit. As a result, it deposited more than $1 billion with a Panamanian payment processor, Crypto Capital Corp. The funds were allegedly confused with corporate and customer deposits and no contract was signed with Crypto Capital. James said that in 2018, Bitfinex and Tether knew or suspected that Crypto Capital had escaped with the money, but their investors were never informed of the loss.

Reggie Fowler, allegedly with ties to Crypto Capital, was indicted on April 30, 2019 for operating an unlicensed money transfer business for virtual money operators. He allegedly failed to return approximately $850 million to an anonymous customer. Investigators also seized $14,000 in counterfeit bills from his office.

Alleged Price Manipulation

Research conducted by John M. Griffin and Amin Shams in 2018 suggests that transactions associated with increases in the quantity of Tether and trading on Bitfinex account for about half of the increase in bitcoin prices by the end of 2017,,·.

Bloomberg News reporters wanted to verify accusations that the price of Tether was manipulated on the Kraken trading platform, and found evidence of price manipulation. The red flags included small orders moving the price as much as large orders, and "strangely specific orders - many to five decimal places, some repeating frequently". These unusually large orders might have been used to signal trade laundering in automated trading programs, according to New York University professor Rosa Abrantes-Metz and former U.S. Federal Reserve Bank examiner Mark Williams.

Depending on Tether's website, Tether may be newly issued, by dollar purchase, or purchased by qualified exchanges and companies, excluding customers located in the United States. Journalist Jon Evans stated that he has not been able to find any publicly verifiable examples of a purchase of Tether, newly issued or repurchased in the year ending August 2018.

J.L. van der Velde, CEO of Bitfinex and Tether, denied the allegations of price manipulation: "Bitfinex and Tether have never engaged in market or price manipulation. Tether's issues cannot be used to raise the price of Bitcoin or any other corner on Bitfinex".

Subpoenas from the Commodity Futures Trading Commission were sent to Tether and Bitfinex on December 6, 2017. Friedman LLP, a former auditor of Tether, has also been subpoenaed. Noble, in turn, used The Bank of New York Mellon Corporation as depositary. As of October 2018, Noble has gone public and would no longer have banking relationships with Tether, Bitfinex or The Bank of New York Mellon. Although Bitfinex does not have the necessary banking connections to accept dollar deposits, the company has denied being insolvent.

Tether announced a new banking relationship with Bahamas-based Deltec Bank in November 2018 through a letter, purportedly from Deltec, indicating that Tether had $1.8 billion on deposit with the bank. The letter contained two paragraphs and an illegible signature, without the name of the author printed on it. A Deltec spokesman refused to confirm the information in the letter to Bloomberg journalists.

Security and liquidity

Tether states that it intends to hold all U.S. dollars in reserve so that it can make customer withdrawals on demand, although it has not been able to meet all withdrawal requests in 2017. Tether claims to make reserve assets transparent through an external audit; however, such audits do not exist. In January 2018, Tether announced that it no longer has a relationship with its auditor. Approximately $31 million in USDT tokens were stolen from Tether in November 2017. A subsequent analysis of the Bitcoin blockchain revealed a strong link between the Tether hack and the January 2015 Bitstamp hack. In response to the theft, Tether suspended trading, and stated that it would deploy new software to implement an emergency "fork" to render all tokens identified by Tether as stolen unusable. Tether said that effective December 19, 2017, the company has reactivated its portfolio services and has begun to process the backlog of pending transactions.

Issues around dollar reserves

A supply chain critic raised questions about the relationship between Bitfinex and Tether... accusing Bitfinex of creating "magical tethers from scratch". In September 2017, Tether published a "memorandum" from an accounting firm that, according to Tether Limited, showed that the tethers were financed entirely by U.S. dollars; however, according to the *New York Times,* independent attorney Lewis Cohen said the document, because of its careful wording, "does not prove that Tether's parts are backed by dollars. Nor do the documents verify whether the balances in question are otherwise affected". The accounting firm specifically stated that "This information is intended solely to assist the management of Tether Limited ... and is not intended to be, and should not be, used or relied upon by any other party. "Tether has repeatedly stated that they will provide audits showing that the amount of outstanding fasteners is individually secured by U.S. dollars on deposit. They have failed to do so. An attempted audit in June 2018 was posted on their website that same month. The law firm Freeh, Sporkin & Sullivan submitted a report that appeared to confirm that the outstanding bonds issued were fully guaranteed in dollars. However, according to FSS, "FSS is not an accounting firm and has not performed the above review and confirmations in accordance with generally accepted accounting principles" and "The above confirmation of bank and related account balances should not be construed as the result of an audit in accordance with generally accepted auditing standards".

Stuart Hoegner, Tether's general counsel, said, "the bottom line is that an audit cannot be achieved. The Big Four companies are anathema to this level of risk. We went for what we think is the next best thing. »

During an investigation into price manipulation by the US Commodity Futures Trading Commission and the US Department of Justice, Phil Potter, Bitfinex Chief Strategy Officer and head of Tether Limited, left Bitfinex in 2018 . According to Bloomberg, the investigation continued on November 20, 2018 and focused on Tether and Bitfinex.

Polkadot

Polkadot is a proposal for an exchange and transfer architecture between several heterogeneous chains, allowing to connect public blockchains with specialized sidechains. Thanks to Polkadot, different blockchains can exchange messages securely and without a trusted third party.

Created by Gavin Wood, co-founder of Ethereum, the protocol raised US$144.3 million in an Initial Coin Offering in October 2017.

The Polkadot project is supported by the Web3 Foundation. The mission of this foundation is to promote the development and use of protocols in the field of decentralized software - in particular those using modern cryptographic methods to ensure decentralization - for the benefit of the stability of the Web3 ecosystem.

Protocol

General description

The Polkadot protocol is designed to become a scalable multichannel technology. Contrary to the usual blockchain implementations, centered around a single blockchain and with various degrees of generalization depending on the applications, Polkadot aims to offer a relay-chain, a base that can host a large number of validatable and globally consistent data structures.

Polkadot can be considered as similar to a grouping of independent blockchains with the exception of 2 important properties: combined security and the ability to perform transactions between chains without the need for trusted third parties.

Polkadot is considered "evolutionary" in its very conception. A problem deployed on Polkadot can be substantially distributed and parallelized over a large number of parachutes. Knowing that all aspects of each parachain can be driven in parallel by different parts of the network, the system is thus considered scalable and extensible on a large scale.

Polkadot is designed to provide the basic elements of an infrastructure, leaving the middleware to manage any application complexity.

Polkadot was created to connect **private/consortium** chains, **public/unauthorized** networks, oracles, and any other Web3 ecosystem technology not yet developed. Through Polkadot's relay-chain, focused on scalability, governance and interoperability, the protocol provides access to an Internet of **independent blockchains that** can **exchange information and perform operations without a trusted third party**.

In general, Polkadot seeks to solve the following problems:

- Interoperability: Polkadot is designed to enable seamless data and resource transactions between applications and smart contracts on different blockchains.
- Scalability: Polkadot allows multiple parachutes to operate simultaneously, each capable of supporting multiple transactions in parallel, the protocol is infinitely scalable.
- Combined security: With Polkadot, network security is shared. This means that each individual channel benefits from the collective security of the network, without having to build everything from scratch and without having to acquire the trust and traction of the network.

History

Dr. Gavin James Wood

Gavin Wood is co-founder and current director of Parity Technologies. He was previously Technical Director and co-founder of the Ethereum project, co-creator of the Ethereum protocol and author of its formal specifications. He also created and programmed the first functional implementation of Ethereum. He designed the Solidity programming language, was the project manager of its Development Environment and the project manager of the creation and implementation of the Whisper protocol. Gavin holds a PhD in Computer Science from York University.

Dr. Wood published Polkadot's whitepaper on November 14, 2017. Responsibility for the protocol was assigned to the Web3 Foundation, created in June 2017.

Initial Coin Offering

Polkadot completed its ICO on October 15, 2017. The sale of the tokens was carried out in the form of a descending auction, known as Dutch style. The initial token sale closed on October 27, 2017, raising a total of ETH 85,331.

Token

Functions

The DOT has 3 main functions, governance, operations and network links.

DOT holders control the entire protocol. All privileges, usually given to minors on other platforms, are given here to the relay participants, including the management of exceptional events such as the evolution of the protocol or its repair.

Game theory encourages token holders to behave honestly. Honest" participants are rewarded through this mechanism, while participants with "bad" behavior will lose their shares in the network. This ensures the security of the network.

New parachutes are added by linked tokens. Unnecessary or obsolete skirts are removed by removing linked tokens. This is a form of Proof of Stake.

The DOT is a native token, the DOTs will be issued when the Polkadot genesis block is created.

Development

The Web3 Foundation commissioned Parity Technologies to build the Polkadot protocol. The work is in progress.

The creation of the genesis block is expected in the third quarter of 2019. Several high-ranking blockchain protocols have already shown interest in Polkadot's parachains, such as Melonport for example.

Cardano

Cardano is an *open source* blockchain, as well as a platform for executing intelligent contracts. Cardano's internal cryptography is called Ada. This project is led by Charles Hoskinson, co-creator of Ethereum. The development of the project is supervised by the Cardano Foundation based in Zug, Switzerland. Cardano is considered by some to be the synthesis of Bitcoin and Ethereum. It is the fourth largest cryptomoney in terms of capitalization, as of February 7, 2021, after Bitcoin, Ethereum, and USDollarTether, but ahead of Ripple.

History

The platform began its development in 2015 and was launched in 2017 by Charles Hoskinson , co-founder of Ethereum and BitShares. According to Hoskinson, he left Ethereum after a dispute over whether to keep Ethereum as a non-profit. After his departure, he co-founded IOHK, a blockchain engineering company, whose main activity is the development of Cardano, alongside the Cardano Foundation and Emurgo. The platform is named after Girolamo Cardano and the cryptography after Ada Lovelace.

The currency made its debut with a market capitalization of $600 million. By the end of 2017, it had a market capitalization of $10 billion and briefly reached a value of $33 billion in 2018 before a general tightening of the cryptography market reduced its value to $10 billion. Cardano claims to overcome existing problems in the cryptography market: mainly that Bitcoin is too slow and rigid, and that Ethereum is not secure and scalable. It is considered as a third generation cryptography by its creators.

Cardano is developed and designed by a team of academics and engineers.

Technical aspects

Cardano uses a proof of participation technology called *Ouroboros*. In comparison, Bitcoin uses the proof of work system; the first blockchain entry and the longest blockchain are used to determine the honest blockchain. Cardano uses only the first blockchain entry, after which the honest chain is proven locally without the need for a trusted third party.

Within the Cardano platform, Ada exists on the settlement layer. This layer is similar to Bitcoin and monitors transactions. The second layer is the calculation layer. This layer is similar to Ethereum, allowing smart contracts and applications to run on the platform.

Cardano has the particularity of not following a white paper. Instead, it uses design principles designed to improve issues faced by other cryptosystems: scalability, interoperability and regulatory compliance. It is funded by an initial cryptomoney offering.

Development

The development of Cardano is divided into 5 stages, called "eras". Each of these eras corresponds to the implementation of new functionalities to the Cardano blockchain, and the development of the blockchain will be considered finished and handed over to the ADA owners at the launch of the fifth era.

Cardano's intelligent contract language allows developers to run end-to-end tests on their program without leaving the integrated development environment or deploying their code.

In 2017, IOHK, the company behind Cardano, helped the University of Edinburgh launch the Blockchain Technology Laboratory. In 2019, Georgia's Minister of Education, Mikhail Batiashvili, and Charles Hoskinson signed a memorandum of understanding with the Free University of Tbilisi to use Cardano and Atala to build a credential verification system for Georgia. In 2018, Cardano has teamed up with the Ethiopian government so that Cardano can deploy its technology in a variety of industries across the country. IOHK donated $500,000 to Ada at the University of Wyoming to support the development of blockchain technology. Shoe manufacturer New Balance will use a blockchain from a distributed ledger to track the authenticity of its latest basketball shoe. The platform will be built on top of the Cardano blockchain.

Stellar

Stellar is an open source payment protocol founded in 2014 by Jed McCaleb and Joyce Kim .

Organization

Its Board of Directors and Advisory Committee members include Keith Rabois, Patrick Collison , Matt Mullenweg , Greg Stein, Joi Ito, Sam Altman, Naval Ravikant and others. '''''

The Stellar Procotole is supported by a non-profit foundation, the Stellar Development Foundation. '''''

This network is non-profit and their platform is open source and decentralized.

How it works

This network has been created to be free to access, and above all easily usable for all income levels and with low transaction costs . Thanks to their intermediate currency, the lumens, a user can send any currency to another person who may have a different currency.

It can make transactions with fiduciary money and with other cryptomoney. This currency is a centralized currency and makes multi-platform transactions and micro-transactions like Ripple, another cryptomony that is also centralized. It is also a payment technology that aims to link financial institutions together and significantly reduce the cost and time for cross-border transfers.

Litecoin

Litecoin is an electronic currency distributed under a free license, inspired by and technically similar to Bitcoin.

Litecoin can work with the same "mining" software as Bitcoin.

Each Litecoin is divided into one hundred million smaller units, defined by eight decimal places.

The *Litecoin* is a registered trademark of the eponymous foundation 111 North Bridge Road Singapore.

History

Litecoin was developed through an *open source* client on GitHub on October 7, 2011 by Charlie Lee, a former Google employee.

The Litecoin code is a modification of the Bitcoin code.

In April 2017, the Litecoin Foundation was established in Singapore with the aim of promoting Litecoin.

On December 15, 2017, the Litecoin exchange rate was added to the Bloomberg Terminal.

On February 18, 2018, Litecoin experienced the first Fork in its history, Litecoin Cash, by a group of independent developers from the Litecoin Foundation. This initiative was strongly criticized by Litecoin's creator, Charlie Lee.

In July 2018, Google added the Litecoin to its currency conversion tool.

General characteristics

Differences with Bitcoin

Litecoin offers some differences from Bitcoin :

- Litecoin's network is designed to create a block every two and a half minutes, rather than every ten minutes for Bitcoin.
- Faster confirmation of transactions.
- Minimal transaction fees.
- The interface was modified to prevent the creation of ASICs, but ASICs were still produced, making mining on standard hardware impractical.
- The mining algorithm can run at the same time and on the same machines used to mine bitcoins.

Mining

The Litecoin can be mined individually or through *pools*.

The currency issue rate follows a geometric series that halves every 840,000 blocks, which occurs approximately every four years until it reaches a total of 84 million LTC.

The SCrypt algorithm used by Litecoin has been designed to be memory intensive so as to hinder the creation of ASICs. Nevertheless, ASICs have been developed for the SCrypt algorithm.

The more stable and high quality a pool is, the more tasks will be assigned to the "miners" in the case of the Litecoin.

Transactions

Transactions are recorded on the Litecoin's specific block chain.

In 2016, the block chain recorded an average :

- 7,500 transactions per day,
- a volume of 10,000,000 Litecoins per day,
- a confirmation time of 2.5 minutes.

In 2018, the Litecoin peaked at 200,000 transactions per day.

In 2020, the Litecoin network had more than 1,400 nodes. Each of them had a copy of all transaction data. This means that the data is not controlled by a single entity, but by a decentralized network.

Exchange places

The Litecoin can be exchanged on different platforms around the world.

Bitcoin Cash

Bitcoin Cash is a cryptocurrency derived from Bitcoin.

As its name implies, BCH is intended to be a version that allows many more transactions per block at a lower price than BTC, branching off from the Bitcoin protocol on August 1, 2017.

Bitcoin Cash is based on the sequential and distributed database technology called blockchain, as described in 2008 by Satoshi Nakamoto.

Background

Since 2014, the number of transactions made in Bitcoin is continuously increasing. The result of this growth is a considerable increase in transaction costs and confirmation time. One possible approach to address this is to increase the block size. Bitcoin Core and a majority of users did not want this increase, so a fork in the road was necessary. Another possible approach, not adopted by Bitcoin Cash, is the use of derivative strings.

On November 15, 2018 BCH will itself experience a fork with the BSV.

Block size

The blocks in the Bitcoin chain were originally limited to 32 MB per block, in order to prevent the chain from becoming too "heavy" for the computers of "small" users; finally, a 1 MB limit was introduced on July 14, 2010. Even with this limit, the original Bitcoin chain currently weighs more than 187 GB; without this limit, the chain could have weighed more than 4 TB, which would have prevented most of the community from having a full Bitcoin node. In the end, the 1MB limit allowed the decentralization of Bitcoin to be maintained.

It was initially planned to be able to possibly adapt this limit. However, this solution, while being the simplest technically and the fastest to implement, requires a bifurcation of the protocol and a break in backward compatibility. This solution was criticized for many reasons, which led to a status quo between 2015 and 2017. Several conferences were held without reaching a general consensus. Since May 15, 2018, the 32 MB limit has been re-introduced for Bitcoin Cash.

SegWit

The implementation of the second solution first required the resolution of the malleability problem. A solution to the malleability problem was proposed: SegWit , a UASF which consists in a backward compatible modification of the Bitcoin protocol. SegWit is an abbreviation for *Segregated Witness*. This modification is the first major modification of the protocol since its invention in 2008 by Satoshi Nakamoto, and it introduces the concept of a derived chain. Indeed, each block is supposed to contain a Merkle tree gathering all the transactions making up the block and their cryptographic signatures, but SegWit separates this cryptographic signature and places it in a derived chain that must be associated with the block for it to be valid. On July 20, 2017, the Bitcoin miners announced that they were 97% ready for Bitcoin Improvement Proposal 91. The proposal was to activate *Segregated Witness on* August [1,] 2017, and maintaining compatibility,,·. On August [1], 2017, the Bitcoin chain protocol implemented *SegWit* .

Difference between Bitcoin and Bitcoin Cash

The Bitcoin Cash protocol is based on the original Bitcoin code but rejects the block size limitation introduced by Satoshi Nakamoto to protect the registry from attacks. It also rejects the SegWit implementation implemented on August 1, 2017.

The capacity problem is solved by the other approach: an immediate increase, at the fork, of the block size to 8 MB, or about 24 transactions per second, and then, later, a complete withdrawal of this limit, which corresponds to a limit of 32 MB, or about 250 transactions per second .

The creation of Bitcoin Cash took place simultaneously with the implementation of SegWit for Bitcoin. This artificial limit of 8 MB per block was then removed on May 15, 2018, leaving only the real limit of 32 MB per block.

To survive the bifurcation with the Bitcoin protocol that implemented SegWit, the difficulty adjustment algorithm was relaxed and then completely modified on November 13, 2017.

Protocols and security

The hash algorithm used by Bitcoin Cash is, as for Bitcoin, SHA-256. As a result, Bitcoin miners can also undermine Bitcoin cash, which increases the risk of attack from the 51% that always falls on the weakest chain.

Bitcoin Cash is nevertheless protected against Replay Attacks which allows co-existence with the Bitcoin chain.

Mining

At the bifurcation with Bitcoin, the size of the mined blocks was a maximum capacity of 8 Mb and the adjustment of the mining difficulty was done every two weeks. Since November 13, 2017, the adjustment of the mining difficulty is done at each block in order to maintain a moving average over 144 blocks of 10 min between each block. In addition, since May 15, 2018, the maximum block size is 32 Mb.

The most efficient type of mining for Bitcoin Cash is mining using ASIC . ASICs capable of mining Bitcoin Cash are also capable of mining Bitcoin because the proof of work is the same.

Transactions and fees

Transactions

Thus, *corners* from different transactions cannot be grouped together. A user receiving several payments will keep as many different amounts in his wallet, even if his software, to make it easier to read, displays them globally. When the user wants to spend them, his software will calculate the best set of input data to transfer to minimize the size of the output data and thus limit transaction costs. Given the very low transaction costs of bitcoin cash, however, it is possible, and very inexpensive, to aggregate many small transactions into a single value.

- *Example: A user receives 13 payments of 1 x 2.3 BCH, 5 x 1.0 BCH, 2 x 0.7 BCH, 1 x 0.5 BCH, 1 x 0.3 BCH, 2 x 0.2 BCH and 1 x 0.1 BCH. His software will then tell him that he has 10.0 BCH.*
- *When they want to spend 3.0 BCH, the best output set will be a combination of the 2.3 BCH and 0.7 BCH previously received.*
- *If he wanted to spend 3.05 BCH, the best output package would be to combine the 2.3 BCH with the 0.7 BCH previously received and split the 0.1 BCH transaction into an output transaction of 0.05 BCH, with the other 0.05 BCH transaction fraction retained in the portfolio.*

Fees

The more a user is willing to pay high transaction fees, the faster their transaction will be processed. Since the blocks in the Bitcoin cash chain are currently large enough to allow miners to undermine all transactions; there is no need to pay a transaction fee for the transaction to be undermined at the next block.

In practice, to be sure that the transaction is confirmed immediately, between 0 and 10 minutes on average, the fees are around 1 satoshis / byte . Thus, in 2018, for a median transaction size of 265 bytes, this represents a cost of approximately 265 satoshis regardless of the amount of cash bitcoins to be transferred.

The larger the input data sets required to complete a transaction, the more bytes are required to encode the transaction and the higher the costs, although the overall amount is virtually zero in the case of Bitcoin Cash.

The software used as a wallet usually calculates the optimal fees to be paid for the transaction to be processed at the time of transfer. These fees vary depending on the number of transactions to be processed at the time of transfer, but they remain virtually zero given the large block capacity. The user alone decides the amount of the transaction fee he is willing to pay.

Buying and selling on exchange platforms

Almost all online cryptographic trading platforms allow you to buy or sell Bitcoin Cash. For example, the following platforms allow you to buy or sell Bitcoin Cash:

- Kraken
- Coinhouse
- Bitfinex
- Bittrex
- Coinbase
- GDAX
- BitMEX
- Binance

- Bitstamp

Dogecoin

Dogecoin is a crypto-coin with an image of the Shiba Inu dog of the same meme "Doge" as logo. Presented as a joke on December 6, 2013, Dogecoin quickly developed its own online community and reached a $60 million capitalization in January 2014.

Compared to other cryptographic currencies, Dogecoin had a fast initial production schedule: 100 billion coins were in circulation by mid-2015, with 5.25 billion additional coins each year thereafter. By June 30, 2015, the 100 billionth Dogecoin had been mined. Although there are few commercial consumer applications, the currency has gained popularity. Dogecoin is an altcoin-type cryptomony.

Overview and history

The Dogecoin was created by Portland-based programmer Billy Markus, who hoped to create a fun crypto-money that could reach more people than Bitcoin. In addition, he wanted to stand out from the controversial story of the other pieces. Meanwhile, Jackson Palmer, a member of Adobe's marketing department in Sydney, was encouraged on Twitter by a Front Range Community College student to make the idea a reality.

After receiving several mentions on Twitter, Palmer purchased the dogecoin.com domain and added a home screen, featuring the coin logo and Comic Sans text. Markus saw the site linked to an IRC discussion forum and set about creating the motto after contacting Palmer. Markus based the Dogecoin on an existing crypto-currency, the Luckycoin, which features a random reward received for operating a block, this feature was then replaced by a static block reward in March 2014. In turn, the Luckycoin is based on the Litecoin which also uses scrypt technology in its proof-of-work algorithm. The use of scrypt means that miners cannot use the SHA-256 mining equipment as they can with bitcoin and that the creation of FPGAs and ASICs dedicated to mining is complicated. The Dogecoin was officially launched on December 6, 2013 . The Dogecoin network was originally expected to produce 100 billion Dogecoins' but it was later announced that the Dogecoin network would produce an infinite number of Dogecoins.

On December 19, 2013, the Dogecoin jumped by almost 300 percent in 72 hours from 0.00026 to 0.00095 $ with a volume of billions of Dogecoins per day. This growth occurred at a time when Bitcoin and many other crypto-currencies were impacted by China's decision to ban Chinese banks from investing in the Bitcoin economy. Three days later, the Dogecoin experienced its first major crash, falling 80% as a result of this event and the presence of large IT pools exploiting the little power needed to mine it.

On December 25, 2013, the first major theft of Dogecoin occurred when millions of coins were stolen during a hack of the Dogewallet online wallet platform. The hacker gained access to the platform's file system and modified its send/receive page to send all the coins to a static address. This hacking incident generated tweets about the Dogecoin, making it the most mentioned altcoin on Twitter at the time, although it was a negative event. To help those who lost funds on Dogewallet after its violation, the Dogecoin community launched an initiative called "SaveDogemas" to help donate coins to those who had been stolen. About a month later, enough money was donated to cover the amount of all the stolen coins. In January 2014, Dogecoin's trading volume briefly surpassed that of Bitcoin and all other encrypted currencies, but its market capitalization remained significantly lower than Bitcoin's. The market capitalization of Dogecoin was still significantly lower than Bitcoin's. The market capitalization of Dogecoin was still significantly lower than Bitcoin's. In April 2015 Jackson Palmer announced that he was taking an "extended leave of absence" from the crypto-currency community. On April 25, 2015, Dogecoin had a market capitalization of $13.5 million.

In January 2018, capitalization reached $2 billion. Capitalization subsequently declined significantly to just over $250 million in January 2019.

Fund Raising

The community and the Dogecoin Foundation have encouraged fundraising for charities and other worthy causes. On January 19, 2014, the Dogecoin community organized a fundraiser to raise fifty thousand dollars for the Jamaican bobsleigh team, which had qualified for the Sochi Winter Olympics but could not afford to go. On the second day, thirty-six thousand dollars in Dogecoin was donated and the exchange rate from Dogecoin to Bitcoin increased by 50%. The Dogecoin community also raised funds for the only Indian athlete present in Sochi, luger Shiva Keshavan.

Doge4Water

Inspired by the fundraising of the Winter Olympics and more modest successes, the Dogecoin Foundation, led by Eric Nakagawa, began collecting donations for the construction of a well in the Tana River Basin in Kenya, in cooperation with Charity: Water. They decided to collect a total of forty million Dogecoins before World Water Day. The campaign was successful, collecting donations from more than four thousand donors, including an anonymous benefactor who donated fourteen million Dogcare.

NASCAR

On March 25, 2014, the Dogecoin community successfully collected 67.8 million Dogecoins to sponsor NASCAR driver

Josh Wise. Wise presented a painting illustration sponsored by Dogecoin and Reddit at the Talladega Superspeedway. On May 4, 2014, Wise and his car were presented for almost a minute, during which race commentators talked about Dogecoin and the participatory fundraising effort, he finished twentieth and narrowly avoided several wrecks. On May 16, 2014, Wise won a spot in the Sprint All-Star Race through an online vote by beating, Danica Patrick, mainly due to the efforts of the Dogecoin and Reddit community. He finished the race in fifteenth position, the last car in the race. In the next race of the Coca-Cola 600, Wise wore a Dogecoin / Reddit.com helmet. Wise later announced that he would use the car again on the Toyota / Save Mart 350 as a thank you to the community and the GEICO 500. He finished twenty-eighth in the race due in part to a refueling problem; he was in twelfth place after a gas stop, but the gas canister did not engage long enough, resulting in a second pit stop that took him to the back of the pack. The developer of the *NASCAR '14* video game *has* announced plans to add the Dogecoin car as a driveable car in an upcoming DLC.

Use and exchange

Several online scholarships offer DOGE / BTC and DOGE / LTC exchanges. Three exchanges, Mengmengbi, Bter and BTC38, offer DOGE / CNY trading. On January 8, 2014, AltQuick.co was the first exchange to launch the DOGE /USD exchange. On January 30, 2014, the Canadian exchange Vault of Satoshi also announced the trading of DOGE / USD and DOGE / CAD. In February 2014, the Hong Kong-based Asia Nexgen Exchange announced that it would support trading of DOGE in all major currencies. China's BTC38 exchange also added its support to the Dogecoin exchange, increasing the 24-hour market capitalization. On the first day of trading, Dogecoin was the second most traded currency on the platform after Bitcoin.

In September 2014, the British Yacuna Stock Exchange began offering DOGE / EUR and DOGE / GBP trading.

On January 31, 2014, the trading volume on the major exchanges was valued at $1.05 million. Market capitalization was $60 million. Three exchanges accounted for the majority of the volume: Bter , Cryptsy and Vircurex . The most traded currency pairs were DOGE / BTC , DOGE / CNY and DOGE / LTC .

Trading of physical and tangible objects in exchange for DOGE takes place in online communities such as Reddit and Twitter, where users frequently share currency information.

The first Dogecoin ATM was introduced at Vancouver's Coinfest in February 2014 . Two Bitcoin ATMs supporting Dogecoins and other altcoins opened in Tijuana on March 17, 2014.

Dogecoin has also been used to try to sell a house and has been used in the pornography and poker industries.

Dogetipbot was a crypto-money transaction service used on popular sites such as Reddit and Twitch.tv. It allowed users to send Dogecoins to other users via commands or via Reddit comments, support for Twitch.tv and Twitter had been discontinued earlier. The service was launched in 2013 on Reddit. The "dogetipbot" brand was officially registered on August 19, 2014. In November 2014, the dogetipbot development team raised $445,000 in venture capital funds. In May 2017, dogetipbot was shut down and taken offline after its creator declared bankruptcy. This left many Dogetipbot users losing their parts stored in the Dogetipbot system.

DogeAPI was the first popular digital wallet for Dogecoins. It was sold in August 2014 to the Blockchain API developer, Block.io.

Evolution of price and capitalization

Mining parameters

The implementation of the Dogecoin differs from the Litecoin by several parameters. Dogecoin has a block time of one minute, in contrast to the 2.5 minutes of Litecoin.

Several cases of using the computer of an employer or a university to exploit Dogecoin were discovered.

The size of the Dogecoin blockchain was 38.8 gigabit in October 2019.

Decentralization

As of October 2018, the number of active nodes on the Dogecoin network was approximately 20,000. Most of the mining work is carried out by mining farms and not individuals.

Number of Dogecoin

Unlike deflationary crypto-currencies, which limit the number of coins that can be produced, the number of Dogecoins that can be produced is unlimited, making it an inflationary coin. The Dogecoin was originally intended to have a limit of 100 billion coins, which would have already represented many more coins than the major digital currencies allowed. In February 2014, Dogecoin's founder, Jackson Palmer, announced that this limit would be removed and that there would be no cap, which should result in a steady reduction in its inflation rate over a long period of time.

Enjoy all our books for free...

  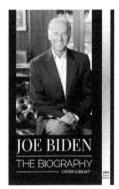

Interesting biographies, engaging introductions, and more.

Join the exclusive United Library reviewers club!

You will get a new book delivered in your inbox every Friday.

Join us today, go to: https://campsite.bio/unitedlibrary

BOOKS BY UNITED LIBRARY

Kamala Harris: The biography

Barack Obama: The biography

Joe Biden: The biography

Adolf Hitler: The biography

Albert Einstein: The biography

Aristotle: The biography

Donald Trump: The biography

Marcus Aurelius: The biography

Napoleon Bonaparte: The biography

Nikola Tesla: The biography

Pope Benedict: The biography

Pope Francis: The biography

Bitcoin: An introduction to the world's leading cryptocurrency

And more...

See all our published books here:
https://campsite.bio/unitedlibrary

ABOUT UNITED LIBRARY

United Library is a small group of enthusiastic writers. Our goal is always to publish books that make a difference, and we are most concerned with whether a book will still be alive in the future. United Library is an independent company, founded in 2010, and now publishing around up to 50 books a year.

Joseph Bryan - FOUNDER/MANAGING EDITOR

Amy Patel - ARCHIVIST AND PUBLISHING ASSISTANT

Mary Kim - OPERATIONS MANAGER

Mary Brown - EDITOR AND TRANSLATOR

Terry Owen – EDITOR

Lightning Source UK Ltd.
Milton Keynes UK
UKHW020640231221
396134UK00010B/811